$hadow Merchant$
Successful Retailing
Without A Storefront

by
Jordan L. Cooper

Loompanics Unlimited
Port Townsend, Washington

$hadow Merchant$
Successful Retailing Without A Storefront
© 1993 by Jordan L. Cooper

Published by:
Loompanics Unlimited
PO Box 1197
Port Townsend, WA 98368
Loompanics Unlimited is a division of Loompanics Enterprises, Inc.

Cover design and illustrations by Jordan L. Cooper

ISBN 1-55950-105-7
Library of Congress Card Catalog 93-79018

Contents

Contents

To Mr. & Mrs. Al

You were always there when we needed you, especially that disastrous day when we all played Russian roulette with pneumonia — and won.

Part One:

General Information

Why Become A Shadow Merchant?

"Boy, did I have a rotten day at work. The boss was on my tail all day long, and for nothing. It's not my fault I can't do the work of three people. If I had some money, I'd start my own business. Then I wouldn't have to take any more of his crap."

How many wives live in dread of hearing that when their husbands come home at night? How many divorces, drunken arguments, beatings, suicides and murders are by-products of an unhappy job situation? In addition to the above extreme examples, how many Americans patiently endure an intolerable job or occupational situation day after day, year after year, while dreaming of owning their own business?

A recent Gallup poll indicated 45 percent of the American work force would change careers if they had the opportunity. Notice the key word is "career," not "job." The percentage of people who would merely like to change jobs within a given field is probably even higher. Even before the collapse of the Soviet Union, it was no secret the USSR was hardly the "worker's paradise" it claimed to be. The good old USA obviously isn't either, although it's still the closest thing to the Promised Land to be found on this planet.

There are millions of Americans who *are* basically happy in their jobs, yet still dream of owning their own business "someday." They look upon it as an opportunity to increase their income, form company policy rather than follow it, and in general escape the corporate bureaucracy and politics of working for someone else... "someday."

Owning your own business is the Great American Dream, but it's realized by relatively few. It *could* become a reality for many if they only knew how to go about it.

What neither group realizes is that "someday" never comes; the only time is *now*. They need to forget the economy is bad, or they're short of money, or simply too busy at the moment. *Now* is the ideal time to start a business, for tomorrow "now" will be gone forever, to be replaced by "someday." After all, Rome wasn't built in a day. Allowing for building permit approval, construction strikes and materials shortages, it took at least a couple of weeks. Corporate giants like Ford, IBM, AT&T and Eastman Kodak weren't built in a day, either. Their founders often worked part-time, on extremely limited budgets. Some failed once, twice, three times or more before finally hitting on the right combination that spelled success.

It takes a lot of time and money to start a small business such as a laundromat, restaurant, shoe store or machine shop. Most people don't have the time or money, but they *do* have the time and money to become a shadow merchant. If the term is unfamiliar to you, don't worry about it. I coined it especially for this book. Reduced to its simplest form, it means exactly what it says: a retailer who doesn't have a storefront, but sells his or her wares in any one or a combination of alternative market locations.

Being a shadow merchant may not offer the prestige of being a store owner, but it definitely offers some advantages that far outweigh the negative aspects. These include:

- Low initial investment.
- Can be done part-time while still holding down a full-time job.
- Low initial overhead, an important consideration even for existing businesses.
- Mobility. If your initial choice of locations is wrong, it's easy to change.
- The flexibility of being able to walk away from the business with a minimum loss if it fails. (Don't let failure discourage you from trying something different later. There is no shame in sincerely trying and failing, only in not having tried at all. Anybody can tell you that Babe Ruth was the home-run king. Few realize he was also the strike-out king.)

With only a small investment of time and money, it's possible to become a shadow merchant *this coming weekend,* or even before. Believe it or not, it can be done in less than an hour, with a total cash investment of under $10. The following examples are based on true stories. They illustrate how two different fellows went about it, with different end results:

Joe was temporarily out of work, but he wasn't out of ideas or a willingness to try something different. He bought one can each of black and white spray paint at the local discount craft supply store. He also bought a set of large number stencils. He then drove around until he found a tract of middle class homes that was perfect for his purpose. Street numbers on the houses were difficult to read and there were no numbers on the curb. After parking his car, Joe approached the first house with spray cans and stencils in hand.

"Good afternoon, ma'am," Joe said when the lady of the house answered the door. "I notice the number on your house is hard to read from the street. I'm out of work and trying to support a family, so if you like, I'll be happy to paint your number on the curb for only a dollar. If you aren't happy with it when I'm done, you don't have to pay me. Is that okay?"

Mrs. Homeowner was aware that people *did* have trouble telling her house from others on the block. She was impressed by the fact Joe was courteous and neatly groomed. She told him to go ahead. When the work was completed, she paid him. Joe thanked her and proceeded to the next house on the block.

Joe didn't get rich that day. He was turned down by several homeowners, but he did show a net profit of $17 for only a couple hours' work. Most important of all, he discovered that he *could* do something to earn a living until he was able to find another job. If Joe should ever find himself out of work again, he will probably say, "Oh, well, I can always go back to painting numbers on curbs."

Bob was an auto mechanic who lived in a winter resort area. He worked for Acme Garage and had steady employment during the winter, but found himself out of work every summer. When winter approached, Acme would always rehire him.

Bob got tired of falling behind on his bills every summer, then playing catch-up in the winter. At the start of one summer lay-off, he decided to clean out his garage and sell the unwanted items at the local swap meet. He was certain he could sell enough to pay at least one full month's bills, thus making it easier to catch up the following winter.

Bob sold enough that weekend to pay his rent and buy a couple weeks' groceries, but realized he had depleted his stock. What would he do next? Somewhat sheepishly, he explained his dilemma to his friend Frank, who offered a solution.

"Try hitting the yard sales next weekend, then take whatever you bought to the swap meet the following weekend," Frank suggested.

Reluctantly, Bob followed Frank's advice. When he counted his receipts the following Sunday afternoon, he realized he had made a substantial profit. He continued to buy at yard sales one weekend, then sell at the swap meet the next. His business and profits increased. When Acme's owner called Bob back to work that winter, Bob told him, "You can't afford me. I'm making more money now than I ever made working for you."

While Joe eventually returned to work at a regular job, Bob elected to remain a shadow merchant. Not only did it pay better than being an auto mechanic, it offered more job security as well. Many occupations in certain areas of the country are subject to seasonal lay-offs such as Bob faced. Affected workers would be wise to follow the examples of Joe and Bob, either temporarily or as a new career opportunity.

If you are out of work and fast running out of both money and job prospects, it may be the luckiest thing that ever happened to you. You can no longer vacillate. You have to act *now!* You may or may not succeed as a shadow merchant, but you owe it to yourself, your family and your creditors to at least try, even if only on a small scale.

I can't guarantee that emulating Joe or Bob will ensure success. I will, however, convey as much useful information as I can to help increase the odds in your favor. There are some procedures which work well for almost anyone, others which are an invitation to disaster. Still other methods will work for one person but not for the next. By learning which are which, you can avoid many costly and potentially disastrous mistakes.

It's not that difficult for anyone who is reasonably intelligent and willing to work to become at least mildly successful as a shadow merchant. That success could eventually lead to far better things. I know of one fellow who failed in his first storefront venture, then became a shadow merchant. He was only modestly successful, so he became a salesman for a company that serviced the retail food industry. He worked hard and did well, occasionally changing jobs during the next 20 years or so while searching for his own "place in the sun." Despite increasing success, he continued to search for that elusive dream, never once giving up. After all, occasional failure was nothing new to him.

He finally found his true niche in life after his 50th birthday, when he once again went into the retail business for himself. His formula for success originated centuries ago, probably at the very dawn of civilization itself, but it still works: give the customer quality, a fair price and service with a smile.

Our former shadow merchant continued to work hard, eventually building a corporate empire that included thousands of stores in the United States, Canada, Europe and Japan. As a boy, he had dreamed of becoming a professional baseball player. Unfortunately, he just wasn't good enough to make it beyond sandlot stardom. But vengeance against unkind fate was sweet. As a successful retailer, he became wealthy enough to buy his own major league team. That team wasn't even a significant part of his livelihood, it was merely his *hobby!*

Very few people could tell you who Ray Kroc was, but virtually everyone is familiar with the company he founded. In the mid-1950s, he began revolutionizing the fast food industry with a little upstart company called McDonald's.

Why Many Businesses Fail
— Before They're Started

Recently my wife and I were driving through one of the main business districts in a large city near our hometown. "I can't believe how many vacant businesses there are here," she remarked. "The economy must be a lot worse than we thought." I then replied that most of those which had closed were probably in trouble even before the economy slowed down. Hard times merely drove the final nail in the lid of the financial coffin.

It's no secret that many small businesses fail, even in the best of times, with restaurants and printers seeming to lead the pack. When times are bad, the rate of closure rises alarmingly. Personally, I'm convinced more small businesses fail before they even open than at any other time, often before they even reach the serious planning stage. This is true regardless of the financial climate of the time. I believe this is so for a number of reasons. Chief among these are:

1. Fear of taking the initial step. (Put another way, this could also be called fear of failure.)
2. Lack of capital.
3. Indecision as to what type of business to start.

Let's look at these roadblocks individually and see what can be done to overcome them:

1. *Fear Of Taking The Initial Step.* A lot of people are afraid to quit their jobs and risk their savings in a business venture. They are also afraid they don't have a head for business matters. These fears are very real and are perfectly justified. The risk of failure can be minimized by becoming a shadow merchant, rather than opening a business in a traditional storefront location. In the event of failure, this minimum risk approach allows you to walk away from the business without incurring disastrous results. After all, you haven't lost everything you had.

2. *Lack Of Capital.* As a shadow merchant, you can open a retail business with a very small investment, as evidenced by the story of Joe in the preceding chapter. You don't need a storefront and inventory the size of the local Sears or WalMart to be successful and show a profit. My wife and I started our business with a total of $43.75 for merchandise. We could ill afford even that amount at the time. Today, we think nothing of risking $500 to $1,000 just to *try*

something new. Occasionally a new item won't sell nearly as well as we expect. More often than not we're very pleasantly surprised with the increase in sales. If we were able to build a full-time business that is our livelihood from such a modest start, others can, too.

3. *Indecision As To What Type Of Business To Start.* Many people who could be in business for themselves create an unnecessary roadblock because they can't decide what type of business to start. It isn't really that difficult to turn off the TV, then sit down and list various possibilities. After all, there are basically only four types of business:

a) **Service**. Janitorial, lawn care, beautician, barber, accounting, music lessons, laundromat, auto repair, etc.

b) **Manufacturing & Production**. Just about everything we use in our everyday lives is made or assembled by *someone*. Many of today's most successful manufacturers started with nothing more than a brainstorm, working in a corner of their living room or garage. We take styrofoam cups for granted, but they were nothing more than an idea in the early 1960s. Two brothers in Phoenix began working with styrofoam beads and a converted pants press from a defunct dry cleaning establishment and a whole new industry was born. Believe it or not, there are thousands of people who are supplementing their income or actually making a living using their own home for manufacturing and production facilities. The proper term for this is cottage industry.

c) **Wholesale**. Some manufacturers wholesale directly to retail outlets. Others sell their product to an independent wholesaler. He in turn resells it to a retailer, usually marking up his cost 20 to 30 percent to cover overhead, profit, etc.

d) **Retail**. A retailer is a person who sells the product to the public or another final buyer. The latter could be a government agency or a large corporation. The list of items that can be sold at retail is virtually endless.

Since this book is devoted exclusively to retailing without a storefront, I won't go into any further detail on the first three categories, other than to mention that some types of businesses overlap. A prime example is my publisher, who fits all four categories. He is in the service business, because he sells useful information in the form of books, which are a manufactured item. He also sells on both the wholesale and retail levels.

In addition to the above reasons why many businesses fail before they start, there are at least seven reasons why some fail *after* they open, sometimes many years later. These are:

1. Undercapitalization.
2. Started at the wrong time or in the wrong location.
3. Lack of knowledge, experience or business acumen on the part of the owner/manager.
4. Overexpansion (or expanding too fast).
5. Poor attitude.
6. Failure to adapt to changing times or conditions.
7. Just plain laziness.

Again, these reasons deserve to be expanded upon individually.

1. *Undercapitalization.* This is probably the single biggest culprit in business failure, at least during the first year. Many first-time business owners assume that if they have good credit and enough money to lease a storefront and stock the shelves, success is assured. They fail to take into account the fact that very few small businesses actually show a profit the first year. There are, of course, noteworthy exceptions, but they are rare.

2. *Started At The Wrong Time Or In The Wrong Location.* Timing and location are far more critical than many people realize. The Great Depression would have seemed like the worst possible time to open a new business or expand an

existing one, yet many large corporations got their start in that era. Their founders succeeded since they had no choice but to succeed or starve. They weren't lulled into a false expectation of instant success merely because of a prosperous world economy. Conversely, the post-World War Two era was an ideal time to start a consumer-oriented business, especially in the Southwest or on the West Coast. Many returning GIs had been temporarily stationed in these areas during the war. For the first time in their lives, they realized they didn't have to fight snow and below-freezing temperatures during the winter months. States like California, Arizona, New Mexico, Texas and Florida experienced a phenomenal increase in population after the war. All these people wanted goods and services which they had been denied during the war years. Homebuilders and auto dealers did especially well.

Even today, timing and location are important factors in business. The proliferation of video rental stores is a direct result of the tremendous increase in home VCR sales in recent years. Not that many years ago, they were something of a novelty in the consumer marketplace.

As for location, a rental firm specializing in wheelchairs, hospital beds and the like might do well in a retirement community. It wouldn't be such a good idea in an area where the average household consisted of a family with small children. Economic, ethnic and racial conditions in a neighborhood are also factors that can influence where a business is located. It doesn't make any sense to open a swank golf or tennis resort in the ghetto, or a Mexican restaurant in San Francisco's Chinatown. Do your homework before deciding what type of business to open in a specific area.

As for timing, try to determine what will be a hot-selling item within the next few months to a year. More money is made at the start of any trend than at any other time. Don't just get in on the ground floor, dig the foundation!

3. *Lack Of Knowledge, Experience Or Business Acumen On The Part Of The Owner/Manager.* Knowledge is power while ignorance is an Achilles' heel that can lead to disaster. There *is* a difference between ignorance and stupidity. The first can be corrected by learning all you can about the business before you start. The latter is a permanent condition that can have terminal results in business. Very few really stupid people succeed in life. Some who just aren't especially bright succeed quite well because they make full use of what brains they have. Business acumen might be equated with a sixth sense, but a certain amount of it can be acquired through experience. You should be able to develop a "feel" for what might sell well, at least in your particular set of business circumstances. You will un-doubtedly make some mistakes, but will also do some things right, surprising even yourself with how profitable a certain item or idea proves to be. Reduced to its simplest terms, business acumen is knowing that if you don't show a reasonable profit for the time, energy and money expended, you are doing something wrong.

4. *Overexpansion (Or Expanding Too Fast).* This particular problem is an easy one to spot in retrospect, but not so easy before the fact. Basically, businesses often expand too quickly when times are good, then don't retrench soon enough when conditions change for the worse. Overexpansion under the wrong conditions almost forced the Coopers into bankruptcy several years ago, but we quickly adapted and survived. The details are to be found in the chapter titled "Other People, Other Units."

5. *Poor Attitude.* Some people mistakenly believe all they have to do is open their own business and they will make a lot of money while only working a few hours per week.

Sorry, but it seldom works that way. Most business people work very hard just to make a living. Even those who achieve great success still have to toil to maintain that success. Competent subordinates can assume a certain amount of responsibility, but the ultimate success or failure of any business rests with the person at the top. As President Harry S. Truman was fond of saying, "The buck stops here."

Some retailers develop a poor attitude based on unrealistic expectations. Remember, instant success doesn't come in a jar, like instant coffee. If you become disgruntled over a seeming lack of progress, it's bound to reflect in your dealings with customers. They will sense your attitude and take their business elsewhere. Force yourself to have a positive attitude if necessary, but always try to project a happy image. After all, you like people who are happy. Others do, too.

6. *Failure To Adapt To Changing Times Or Conditions.* The least successful shadow merchants I know are those who are selling the same items in the same locations as they did five or even ten years ago. The most successful are the ones who recognize the need to change and who constantly upgrade, expand and revitalize their inventory. This subject will be covered far more thoroughly in the chapter entitled "When To Diversify."

7. *Just Plain Laziness.* Basically, there are three types of laziness: psychological, mental and physical. A person can be reasonably intelligent and healthy and work hard at their job, yet have no ambition to go any further in life than their present position. Such people are psychologically lazy, which in itself isn't necessarily a bad trait. There is a definite demand for people who are competent, good workers and no job threat to their boss. They are an asset to their employer and may well work for the same company

from the time they get out of school until they retire. They may never reach their full potential, but they don't waste their lives, either. The mentally lazy are those who have an intelligent mind, but refuse to use it. They *are* wasting their full potential, but they may still function adequately enough to be an asset to their employer. Many people who are physically lazy suffer from poor health, and I can sympathize with them. Often a minimum effort is literally all they can achieve. However, there are far too many healthy people who are physically lazy. They waste their entire lives by expending as little effort as possible. If they work at all, they turn in only a marginal performance. Fortunately, some lazy people are honest enough to admit it, even to themselves, and force themselves to perform at somewhere near their maximum potential. They deserve a certain amount of credit for recognizing their fault and trying to correct it. If you know you are lazy and are still too lazy to force yourself to succeed, you will probably be wasting your time if you read any further. Laziness belongs in the welfare line, not in the business world.

The Winning Combination

Becoming successful as a shadow merchant is no big deal. All it takes is to be in the right place at the right time with the right merchandise at the right price. A simple combination, right? After all, it's only four numbers instead of the six or seven needed to win a lottery. Unfortunately, it isn't really that simple. You can have three of the four down perfect, but if that all-important fourth number is wrong, it can spell D-I-S-A-S-T-E-R with a capital B as in *bankruptcy*.

As in any endeavor, however, the more knowledge you have beforehand, the better your chances of success. In the following chapters, I will try to provide enough information so you can at least come close to achieving the winning combination at the very start.

It shouldn't be any great secret that certain types of merchandise will sell well in one area and not in another. Based on observation, however, this seems to be the best-kept secret in the country. I have seen countless swap meet vendors who were practically starving because they were trying to sell the wrong item to the wrong clientele. In many cases, they could have gone just a few miles down the road and done well with the same merchandise but an entirely different clientele. Every selling location is different, and can even vary from one day or season to another.

A couple of examples should illustrate some of these differences adequately.

Recently, my wife and I visited a new swap meet in a large city near our hometown. We had heard a lot of interesting rumors about it, but knew from past experience there is no substitute for doing your own on-site evaluation. It was a hot, muggy Saturday morning, so the crowd wasn't very large. Its composition was approximately 80 percent Hispanic, 20 percent Anglo. One vendor informed us the crowd is much larger on Sundays, and is approximately 60 percent Hispanic, 40 percent Anglo. With this mix, we weren't surprised to see a fairly large number of vendors selling used goods and only a limited selection of new merchandise. We have worked heavily Hispanic markets in the past, and could almost guess what the real pros would be selling: 14 karat gold jewelry (several stalls), Spanish-language cassette tapes, children's clothing, stereos, car seat cushions and cheap toys. Only one stall featured conservatively-styled women's clothing. A T-shirt dealer prominently displayed popular designs that would have been poor sellers at another swap meet just a few miles away. We didn't see any really nice, high-ticket decorator items, but knew from past experience some of the clientele of this market would buy them for Christmas gifts. Since most of them have a lower than average income, they also tend to start their Christmas shopping early. This allows them to spread the economic impact over a longer period of time.

The following evening, we walked through our hometown swap meet just to see what was happening. Before presenting our observations, a little background on the area is in order.

The year-around population of this city (if you can call it that) is 18,000. In the summer the area is about as depressed as can be found. It's a standing joke that there are only two sources of income in the summer: Those who aren't on welfare are on the city payroll. This is a slight exaggeration, but basically true, with the top city officials being paid almost as much as the governor of the state.

In the winter, the economic picture brightens as thousands of winter visitors (affectionately called snowbirds) flock to the area. The RV parks prominently display "No Vacancy" signs and the dinner theaters have lines of customers standing outside the door an hour or two before they open. Supermarket parking lots, which are virtually empty during the summer months, are jammed with Cadillacs and motor homes sporting out-of-state license plates.

Needless to say, the merchandise offered at the local swap meet clearly reflects this change in the economic climate. In the summer, about 50 percent of the vendors are "junkers" trying to dispose of unwanted items. The other 50 percent are mainly the bottom echelon of the pros, selling socks, cheap plastic jewelry and Taiwan imports. In the winter, the *real pros* move in. Some come from the fair circuit in the Midwest, others from their gift shops in summer resort areas. There isn't a single Indian jewelry dealer there during the summer. In the winter, there are 48 of them. There are also a number of vendors selling high-ticket Southwestern fashions and large decorator items. A few winter vendors literally have semi trailers full of merchandise parked in their spaces, and *still* sell out of certain items in a single weekend. What would be a good day's gross sales in the summer is a good hour's sales in the winter. It's not surprising that a national association of vendors rated it one of the top ten swap meets in the nation.

My wife and I were lucky enough to discover it right at the height of the winter season several years ago. We had just gotten started in the business and had drawn a blank at another swap meet the weekend before. However, a vendor there suggested we try the market which he had heard was so good for tourist-type items. We decided to heed his advice.

Our Indian art was a smash hit. We sold 11 out of 14 items in less than two hours. Deciding to gamble, we took the money we had set aside to pay the following month's bills and invested it in more Indian art from the same source. We *thought* we had enough inventory to sell Friday, Saturday and Sunday. As it worked out, we took the following Sunday off. We weren't lazy, just out of merchandise! We bought even more the next week. The same scenario happened again, and yet again the following weekend. It was obvious we had found the winning combination for us. The only bugaboo was that we found it at the end of the winter season instead of the beginning. However, it did work for us long enough to clearly indicate we *could* make a living as shadow merchants.

The following winter, we commuted each weekend from our hometown 150 miles away. We have since relocated to within a few miles of the swap meet, forsaking a rural area we loved for a large metropolitan area that is less than ideal. That's the price we had to pay in order to make a living. However, we have the consolation of living in the local equivalent of the country club area (along with several other vendors). It doesn't really cost us much more than it would to live in the slums nearer the swap meet, and our address is definitely a plus when dealing with the higher class winter clientele. It's a lot of fun to watch someone's eyebrows rise as they say, "You live out *there*? That's a nice area."

The two swap meets listed above should serve as good general examples of how the winning combination works. However, the selection of merchandise and location are so important in themselves as to require further amplification. The following chapter will deal specifically with merchandise and pricing. Part Two of this book will be devoted entirely to some of the various types of location options available to shadow merchants. These are by no means limited to swap meets or the other locations I describe. They are limited only by your imagination and particular situation, as well as certain regional factors. Don't be afraid to try a type of location not listed herein, it might be the critical fourth factor in your favor!

Sell What You Like

Some individuals are born salespeople, they can sell just about anything equally well. Others are good at selling one item, mediocre at another. A perfect example is car salesmen. The "Hiya, pal, I are your good ol' country boy and I are gonna sell you a car today" approach may work on a used car lot in Hayseed Junction. It requires an entirely different technique to sell a Mercedes to a doctor, stock broker or banker in Blueblood City. These individuals don't need to be sold, they deserve to be treated with some respect as they walk into the dealership with the intention of buying in the first place.

At the bottom of the sales aptitude ladder there are, unfortunately, some individuals who just don't have much natural sales ability. They are usually shy and have to force themselves to even speak to a customer, let alone try to close a sale. For them, it's a definite plus if they can sell something they really like. After all, they have to show some enthusiasm or the potential customer will walk away with empty hands.

My wife and I are good examples of how this works. She is the gregarious type (some might say pushy) who has no trouble approaching strangers. I would probably qualify as a latent hermit. Our difference in types was borne out during our first few weeks as shadow merchants. Many of the customers who bought our merchandise were elderly women. My wife had no trouble selling to them. Even though I was enthusiastic about the merchandise, they would walk away if I approached them. "Little old ladies are often intimidated by a man trying to sell to them, especially if he's taller than they are," my wife explained. She was probably right, but her evaluation sank in a little too deeply. Even today, I have trouble making the initial contact with older women. Fortunately, I come alive when a potential customer is a biker type (either male or female), someone in military uniform, or a desert rat who obviously left his burro tied at the front gate. I can't see myself intimidating any of these people, especially a six-five, 300-pound biker!

I also have trouble approaching someone who is looking at a type of merchandise we have carried for some time. I simply dread answering the same dumb questions I've answered at least 10,000 times in the last few years. On the other hand, I'm practically eager to approach a customer if they are looking at a new item we have just added to our inventory. My enthusiasm for that item is still fresh, and since it's new I want to give it a fair chance. I'm sure other shadow merchants also have trouble when the warranty on their enthusiasm for older merchandise expires. This alone is ample reason for changing inventory occasionally. There are other, more important reasons for changing it as well. They will be covered in the next chapter.

No salesperson is going to be filled with enthusiasm every single day, no matter how much they like selling, but it certainly helps if they can sell something they like and which truly interests them.

An auto mechanic would be much happier selling tools or auto accessories than ladies' foundation garments. He will already be familiar with them and will be able to discuss them knowledgeably with customers. If his hobby is model trains or radio-controlled airplanes, he might want to consider selling hobby supplies. A beautician is better qualified to sell hair care and beauty supplies than tires. She could also sell ladies' fashions and accessories. She *should* be able to tell what styles and colors would be complementary to any given combination of skin tones, hair color and general physical appearance. If a customer with the body of a beer keg and legs like an elephant's is considering a mini-skirt and skimpy top, she could tactfully direct that lady to a style that is more suited to her general build.

A retired professional athlete should definitely consider selling sports-related items. He will obviously be an expert on his particular sport. His name alone will be a drawing card. Customers just *know* he has a lot of interesting stories to tell (Momma Dimaggio made the best ravioli of any Italian mother in baseball, etc.). People also like to brag about the fact they met a former celebrity ("Remember Zucchini who played fullback for the Rams back in '78? He sold me that warm-up jacket.").

One fellow I know sells Omnichords at the local swap meet in the winter, then takes them back to Nebraska in the summer. He demonstrates his product while singing a repertoire of popular Country & Western standards. A crowd usually gathers around, as he has a voice and style reminiscent of the late Marty Robbins. As a lucrative sideline, he sells cassette tapes that he recorded in a professional studio. Obviously, sounding like the great Marty isn't the worst fate that could befall a country singer!

The list of occupational and personal interest-related items which can be sold by shadow merchants is limited only by one's imagination and willingness to do a little homework. When the list is expanded to include retail merchandise in general, it becomes virtually endless. However, possibilities can be broken down into three main groups: manufactured goods, handcrafted items and used goods. Each deserves individual attention.

Manufactured Goods

"I can get it for you wholesale" is a famous old Jewish saying that is quite true. With the exception of certain items they handcraft themselves, virtually anything that can be sold by shadow merchants can be bought wholesale — somewhere. The secret is to find out where, but it usually isn't all that difficult.

Several years ago, we met a couple who had recently lost their source of doggie chews when the manufacturer went out of business. All winter long, they kept whining, "We lost our doggie chews." My wife told them there were several sources listed in the trade publications which were available at the swap meet office. They never followed up on her suggestion. After all, it was much easier to just keep whining and let a couple of other vendors hand them merchandise to sell on commission. That way they didn't have to invest any of their own money and could let someone else do a lot of preliminary work for them.

By contrast, the following summer we met a vendor who sold framed art prints at another swap meet. He told us he was overstocked at the moment and was looking for someone he could wholesale to. We met him at his warehouse and examined the prints, which were of good quality. He quoted us a whole-sale price and told us what he normally sold them for retail. We told him we would get back to him and drove home.

We didn't know the name of the manufacturer, but had mentally noted a trade name on the corner protectors which we suspected was also the company name. From the course of our conversation with this fellow, we were fairly certain he bought them in the Los Angeles area. Within minutes after we returned home, my wife had gotten a telephone number from the infor-mation operator, had placed a call to the factory and had a color catalog on the way to us. Obviously, if she could do that in a matter of minutes, the doggie chew dimwits could have found a new source in the course of a whole winter. Is it any wonder people say the difference between the haves and have-nots is often the difference between the dids and did-nots?

If there is a large swap meet in your area, it's as good a place as any to see the different types of merchandise generally sold by shadow merchants. Try to visit it on a busy day, when it will have the greatest number of vendors. The variety of merchan-dise will amaze you, especially if the customers are a good cross section of the population in regard to age, race, economic background, etc. Observe which vendors are busy and which aren't. Check each row again later in the day. Some vendors will be busiest in the morning, others in the afternoon. A few will be busy all the time, others only occasionally. Take note of the ones who are busiest, what they sell, their prices, and the general appearance of their stalls. Usually, the busiest vendors will be those who have the most attractive displays, which speaks well for their merchandising skills.

One fallacy to which both new shadow merchants and veterans alike can fall victim is the assumption that if a lot of vendors are selling a particular item, it must be profitable. This isn't necessarily true. A lot of competition usually generates a price war with everyone losing in the end. Let's assume, for example, a certain item wholesales for $2.50. It is common practice for both stores and shadow merchants to set a retail price by doubling the wholesale cost to $5. This is called a keystone. A three-time markup, or $7.50, is called a tristone. This may look like a profit of $2.50 or $5 respectively, but it isn't. When all operating expenses such as rent, salaries, shipping, etc., are deducted, the actual profit is considerably lower.

Some retailers believe they can operate on a low profit margin and make up the difference in volume. This practice may work well for large discount chains that get a wholesale price break when buying in quantity, but it's disastrous for the smaller operator. Some shadow merchants who don't realize this take in literally thousands of dollars each week, yet they eat beans because that's all they can afford. For the little guy, there is simply no future in selling an item that wholesales for $2.50 at a retail price of $2.75. A friend of mine is quick to point this out to those who brag about their large grosses. "Never mind what your gross is, what's your net? N-E-T, net," he says. Wallace knows exactly what he's talking about. At the end of the selling day, he actually puts more money in his pocket than many others whose gross sales exceed his by 10 or 20 times.

Needless to say, the best profit margin can be achieved with merchandise for which there is no competition. It takes more effort to locate its sources, which further decreases the risk of competition. Very few shadow merchants are willing to do that much extra work.

Wholesale trade shows are excellent sources for unusual merchandise. You will often find top-selling items your competitors don't even know exist. These shows aren't open to the general public, but usually all it takes to get in the exhibit hall is a sales tax license and business card. We attend at least two of these shows in our area each year, even if it means missing some good selling days.

The first show is a general gift show during the first weekend in August. The last one we attended featured over 1200 booths, with many sales reps exhibiting new items available for shipment just prior to the heaviest pre-Christmas buying period. We were just getting into the business when we attended our first gift show several years ago. The experience was traumatic, as we tried to spend some time in every single booth in just one day. We stumbled out of the show in a state of shock, only vaguely aware of what we had just seen.

The following year, we tried a different approach. My wife started at one end of the hall while I started at the other. We met in the center within an hour, having jotted down the booth numbers of exhibits which appealed to us. We were then able to return to them and study the merchandise in a leisurely manner.

This year, we tried yet a third approach and found it to be best of all. On Friday, we walked the entire show, stopping briefly at the 25 or 30 booths which appealed to us. We are now experienced enough to know which types of merchandise will complement our present inventory and which won't, so it was relatively easy to separate the two. We stayed home on Saturday, studying catalogs and price sheets and composing tentative orders. We returned to the show on Sunday to place our orders and reexamine certain items we had given only a cursory inspection on Friday. While this approach meant sacrificing an entire selling weekend, it was worth it. The profit we made on just one new line the first weekend we had it more than offset any we lost the weekend of the show, when our sales would probably have been slow anyway.

The second show we attend faithfully is the semi-annual Indian Arts and Crafts Association (IACA) show at the end of

October. Unlike the gift show, this one is devoted entirely to Native American arts and crafts, which are the mainstay of our business. This show is also different in that it features many one-of-a-kind items you can purchase right at the show. The show's timing is almost perfect, as it allows us to build our inventory immediately prior to the first major influx of winter visitors. It also enables us to meet and get to know numerous outstanding Indian artists and craftspeople we would otherwise know by reputation only. Most are very nice people who will go out of their way to accommodate their customers. The only problem with this show is we never seem to have enough money to buy all the wonderful things we just *know* we can sell at a good profit!

If there aren't any wholesale shows in your area, don't despair. Wholesale ads for all types of general merchandise can be found in the trade publications which are usually available in swap meet offices. These also include listings of some of the larger trade shows which may not be too far away. There are also numerous publications devoted to specific interests which *aren't* found in swap meet offices, but which are gold mines for sources. These include such diverse titles as *Lapidary Journal* (for the gem and mineral trade), *Shotgun News* (for sporting goods), *The Indian Trader* (the single best source for *anything* pertaining to American Indians), etc. Many of these can be purchased at retail shops catering to specific interest groups. Some specialty publications will be listed in the current edition of *Writer's Market*, which can be found at most public libraries. If all else fails, let your fingers do the walking through the Yellow Pages. Just check the listings for wholesalers under the specific category in which you are interested.

Handcrafted Items

An old saying goes, "There's nothing new under the sun." Maybe not, but there are certainly numerous ways of presenting old items in a new light. Many are yet to be discovered, awaiting only an imaginative crafter with enough gumption to give them a try. Even if an idea isn't entirely new, it's *still* new to someone who has never seen it before.

Handcrafted items have enjoyed a resurgence in popularity in recent years, for a number of reasons. Some people view them as a viable method of protesting an age ruled by modern technology. Others feel that handcrafted items are superior in quality to those which are mass-produced. Still others derive joy from owning something which is unique. Even if the crafter reuses a pattern or idea, the next one they produce won't be exactly like the last.

For whatever reason, handcrafted items are big business today, when viewed as a whole. Many artists and crafters earn a substantial supplemental income or even a comfortable living through their individual talents. How many frustrated accountants, dentists, plumbers or assembly line workers would rather spend their time making artificial floral arrangements, solid oak furniture or one-of-a-kind fashion accessories? The answer is quite a few, and most of them could be doing just that if they really tried.

The list of handcrafted items which can be made and sold profitably is virtually endless. A few possibilities include jewelry, designer clothing, leather goods, wooden toys, incense, stuffed animals, pottery, Indian artifacts and musical instruments. Patterns for some of the above can be found in hobby magazines or can be purchased at craft supply stores. You can also make your own patterns for something that is really unique.

Cowboy bandannas have probably been around in one form or another ever since the first cowboys trailed a herd of long-horns north from Texas. Despite their practical application, they had become basically a ho-hum item nobody noticed at swap meets or in Western stores. After all, they had been around for better than a century, but who cared? Then along came an enterprising gal with an idea and a pair of scissors. By cutting the border to resemble fringe, then adding a few beads and nickel silver conchos, she turned bandannas into a fashion sensation that spread all the way to the East Coast and Hawaii. Another lady copied her idea, then adapted it to sweatshirts to create yet another top-selling fashion. Just where it will end is anybody's guess, but Old West-inspired fashions are just one of the many kinds of handcrafted items which are making a lot of money for a lot of crafters.

If you are one of those people who is "all thumbs" and can't make something yourself, it's still possible to sell handcrafted items made by someone else. In the past year, my wife and I have availed ourselves of the talents of several individual artists and crafters in addition to using our regular wholesale sources of Indian handicrafts. This gives us a wide variety of merchandise. It also assures us of a steady source in case one supplier moves out of the area or breaks an arm and is unable to work for awhile. We've found these people at arts & crafts shows, swap meets and boutiques. One lady who makes beauti-ful Indian artifacts contacted us through our ad in the Yellow Pages. Another works for us as a salesperson during the winter months. If you don't know where to look for crafters, it's only because you aren't really looking. They *are* out there!

Last but certainly not least, we have also begun selling my original oil paintings. That sideline started when I was cleaning out the garage a couple of years ago. I hadn't painted in years, but found some blank canvases and my box of paints. I thought a couple of paintings might help fill wall space when we ran we ran short of our regular wall hangings, so I put in a couple of afternoons at my easel. My first oil sold in just a couple of weeks, and I've been doing them in my limited spare time ever since. We'll never get rich selling them, but the profit margin is certainly appealing, which brings up another point. When selling your own art and handicrafts, be sure to figure a decent wage for your time into the price structure. There is no point in giving your time and energy away, even if you do enjoy what you're doing.

Whether you plan to sell manufactured goods or handicrafts as a shadow merchant, I have one word of caution if you can't decide between two specific items: All other factors being equal, choose the one which is less bulky and which can be set up and torn down in the least amount of time. After all, a good inventory of jewelry and an effective display for it can be carried in a Toyota hatchback. It takes a truck the size of a U-Haul to carry a selection of baby cribs or bicycles. Loading and unloading them is much harder work and also takes a lot longer.

Used Goods

Although lacking in prestige, the sale of used goods at the local swap meet is always a viable option. There is a constant demand for used items of every description in good condition, especially in economically depressed areas.

Your initial inventory can come from your own home. Clean out the closets, attic, garage and storage room. Make sure small appliances are in working order. Clean any items that are dirty. If something is broken, either fix it or throw it away. Items which are clean and operable will have more eye appeal, will sell faster and bring a higher price than junk which should simply be thrown away in the first place.

Once your supply of used goods begins to dwindle, look around for other sources of merchandise. There are many regular dealers who sell nothing but used items year after year. They canvas other vendors early in the day or right at closing time. They may buy items individually or make an offer for an entire lot. Some make a habit of visiting yard sales on Saturday, then reselling their purchases at the swap meet on Sunday. Others regularly visit mini-storages and bid on items which are being sold to help pay back rent. One fellow I know does this regularly, and claims he often makes a profit before he even leaves the storage lot. He will simply start opening boxes to examine his purchases. Other bidders will come up and say, "I could use that. What will you take for it?"

Some vendors specialize in certain types of used goods, such as baby clothes, vacuum cleaners, antiques & collectibles or golf clubs. Others will sell anything they can buy cheaply and resell at a profit. One lady I know paid less than a dollar for a piece of antique glassware in the morning. That afternoon, she resold it to an assistant curator of the Smithsonian at a handsome profit. Such quick, lucrative sales are rare, but they do happen!

As with new merchandise, it's possible to become overburdened with size and weight when selling used goods. My wife and I were reminded just how ridiculous this can get one summer weekend last year. We noticed a lot of people turning to stare at a pickup that was pulling a flatbed trailer slowly down the aisle. There was nothing unusual about this sight — except for what was on the flatbed. It was a full-sized swimming pool, complete with diving board!

When To Diversify

The season for our winter market officially starts the first weekend in October. We don't normally work it until Thanksgiving weekend because there simply isn't much demand for Indian art until then. Vendors who sell kitchen gadgets, clothes, Indian jewelry and sunglasses *can* do well in October, so some of them do set up at the beginning of the season. Their merchandise is something the snowbirds can buy and use as soon as they arrive. This year, we decided to give the market a try in October. We've been there ever since, as our sales were far better the first weekend than we dared hope. No, the snowbirds didn't start buying Indian art early, but they *did* buy from our featured display. We grossed more in the first four selling days than we did in four weekends five years ago — simply because we had diversified in the meantime. Just how we did this will be revealed later, but first a little background on diversification is in order.

We were driving home from an off-season market last fall when I was suddenly struck by a rather grim thought concerning another couple who sell at our winter market. "You know, Fred and Nancy are in for a real shock this winter," I commented.

"Why do you say that?" my wife asked sleepily.

"This is the third year they'll be selling the same thing," I answered. "As far as we know, they haven't made any changes at all in their merchandise."

"Golly, I hadn't thought of that," she said, suddenly wide awake, "but you're right."

My sense of foreboding about Fred and Nancy was confirmed a few days later by a mutual friend. "Everybody's complaining about how slow it is," he said, "but Fred and Nancy are *really* hurting. They're running off more than $1,000 per weekend from last year."

Fred and Nancy had done extremely well with their unique product the first year they sold it. The following year they did almost as well. Without realizing it, they became complacent, expecting the gravy train to last forever. They unwittingly fell victim to what I call the "third year blahs." In other words, they had nothing new to appeal to customers, who would walk by their stall and tell themselves, "Ho-hum, same old thing." In fact, I've heard customers make that comment about the swap meet in general. As mentioned previously, the vendors who complain the most about sales going down each year are the ones who sell the exact same thing year after year. Invariably the ones who say their business has increased are those who have made significant changes in their merchandise.

It may sound strange, but one of the worst things that can happen to any business is outstanding initial success. We learned that the hard way, as did Fred and Nancy. I'm a firm believer in maintaining a steady course of action so long as it works, but altering course drastically once the original fails.

The first winter my wife and I were shadow merchants, it seemed we could do no wrong. We had a unique product which sold well. Our sales increased almost directly in proportion to inventory expansion early in the season. While other, long-established vendors were complaining about poor sales, we were setting records almost daily (it's *real* easy to do when you're starting at the bottom). When that happens, it's easy to assume you're doing everything right.

We didn't realize a good bit of our success was simply because we had a desirable product customers hadn't seen before. Our sales would have undoubtedly been even better if we had been able to get enough product to satisfy the demand. Our sales were limited by what our Indian artists could produce in a given period of time. We had to make a 400-mile round trip every week to pick up merchandise. More than once, we were only able to spend half as much on our inventory as we had budgeted — simply because of a lack of product! "You certainly don't have much of a selection," customers would say on Sunday afternoon. About all we could do was tell them to see us *early* the following weekend, when we would hopefully have enough merchandise to satisfy them.

With business booming, we decided to branch out into a higher price bracket. Our initial offerings at the start of the season were, quite frankly, of tourist-grade souvenir quality, even though they were far better than what our competitors were selling. We added a few more expensive works by a well-known artist and they sold well. A few weeks later, we decided to try a single piece by his brother-in-law, who at that time was the very best in the business. That particular piece carried a $500 price tag. We never expected to sell it, but wanted to use it as an example of truly outstanding quality. It sold less than three hours after we put it on display. Within a few weeks, we were selling almost everything that artist was able to produce. By the end of the season, we had sold 22 of his works, although only a handful were in the $500 price range.

As we entered our second winter season, we fully expected our sales to show an increase over the first. "After all," we said, "we spent a lot of time last year familiarizing people with our product and creating a market for it. This year, customers will be looking for us and will buy even more."

It came as a rude awakening when our sales went down. In our case, the third year blahs struck a year early. We've since learned this isn't uncommon. We knew something was obviously wrong, but each month we could find a logical reason why sales were down for that particular month.

In November and December, we lost seven prime selling days due to rain. In January, we were unable to get any work from our most popular artist. The decrease in sales almost exactly matched the amount of his work we had sold the preceding January. By February, we were so busy we simply didn't have time to look for the cause of the problem. We had set up a second unit at the same swap meet and were also supplying a third in another city. "At least the other units are taking up the slack," we said. In March, our sales were almost identical to the preceding year, which was surprising. I strongly suspected our second unit was siphoning sales away from us (more on that fiasco in the next chapter).

Several years later, a comparison of all the winter seasons to date proved conclusively the second unit *did* cut into our sales, and deeply. It was impossible to determine earlier due to the limited information on hand. There was, however, another factor which contributed significantly to our decrease in sales. If we had only realized it at the time, we might have been able to diversify enough to more than offset any sales we lost to the second unit. It might have meant short-changing them some, but again, that wouldn't have been such a bad idea, either.

We had begun keeping a detailed inventory sheet of sales early in our first season, and continue to do so even today. Its original purpose was to aid us in determining what to restock for the following weekend. However, its greatest value became apparent at the end of the second season.

When I was finally able to compare the sheets for both seasons, it was like a kick between the eyes. Although overall gross sales on just our unit had only dropped 16 percent, sales of the souvenir-type art were down 56 percent. Comparing the totals for each year in the different price ranges showed there was obviously a trend away from items in the $10 to $40 price range. Sales of individual items priced above or below that range hadn't changed all that much, except for significant increases on a couple of items. I made a mental note of this trend and watched it daily throughout the following summer. It held true. If we sold an item priced between $10 and $40, it was almost invariably part of a multiple sale totaling more than $40.

At the end of the summer, we mentioned this trend to several shopkeepers we knew. "You know, I think I've noticed that, too," a couple of the more astute commented. That was several years ago, and we *still* see that trend to some extent. Perhaps it's an indication of the overall economy. People with very little money will spend up to $10 for a nice souvenir or inexpensive gift. Those who have money think nothing of spending over $40.

Based on two years' experience, we predicted sales of the souvenir-type art would probably be even lower the third year. It was readily apparent we would need to diversify, but what direction should we take? The answer came in a rather unexpected manner.

A friend who worked our winter market suffered a bad fall at the end of the season and had to spend several months recuperating. As a favor, he asked us to take some of his mineral specimens and semi-precious gemstone jewelry to our summer location. We weren't particularly enthusiastic about the idea, but agreed to help him out. Since rocks and minerals were a far cry from what we had been selling for two years, we wondered if the change would be appropriate.

Much to our surprise, his merchandise sold almost as well as our Indian art. On some days, it sold better. Our commission on it was a welcome addition to our then-lean summer income. It's not surprising that we suddenly remembered a regular wholesale supplier had often suggested we carry certain items similar to our friend's. We had declined in the past, but our newfound success made us reconsider in his favor. We invested a grand total of $13.50 in some fool's gold and other specimens to try the following weekend.

With that humble beginning, what we jokingly called our "nickel and dime" table was born. Sales were, however, anything *but* nickel and dime. Our initial investment returned a net profit to us the first weekend that far exceeded our wholesale cost. We began expanding the nickel and dime section as rapidly as our limited finances would permit. Although we were barely able to buy groceries at the time, we instituted what I called our "under $20" policy. In other words, if we could try a new nickel and dime item for under $20, we did it. This was fairly easy to do, despite the fact many wholesalers require a $50 or $100 minimum order. We simply bought from suppliers with whom we already dealt. Sales on a few items were disappointing, but others were quite profitable.

Foremost among the "winners" were desert roses. These are, quite simply, rocks that look strikingly like real roses. The first weekend we had them, we sold every one we had. Needless to say, we invested every dime we could spare in more desert roses for the following weekend — and raised our retail price on them. They continued to sell very well throughout the summer and into the fall.

By the time we returned to our winter location, the nickel and dime setup occupied about one-third of our entire table space. About half of that was devoted exclusively to desert roses. Since our initial supplier was unable to meet our demand for desert roses, we were also buying them from two additional sources. These suppliers made suggestions of their own as to other items to sell. Again, some items sold rather poorly while others did quite well. We eliminated the losers and expanded the winners, learning as we went.

One of the first things we learned was that most people had no idea what desert roses were. The first two weekends, we were hoarse by the end of each day from explaining them to customers. A quick trip to the library provided all the information we needed. Armed with notes from several sources, including *Encyclopedia Britannica*, I wrote a short explanatory paragraph and rushed it off to the local printer. The third weekend of the season, we had a stack of nice yellow cards to give each customer who bought a desert rose. My research paid off in several ways, not the least of which was oneupsmanship. Within weeks, another vendor who had noticed our success began selling desert roses. She made a point of telling customers my wife was lying when she said desert roses grew (a perfectly acceptable term for their geological formation). "Well, isn't it nice that dumb broad knows more than *Encyclopedia Britannica?*" we replied.

Of course, you can't sell a new item if potential customers don't know you have it. We solved that problem by running an ad for the desert roses on the swap meet's PA system. The ad read something like this:

A ROSE IS A ROSE, EVEN WHEN IT'S A DESERT ROSE. WHAT IS A DESERT ROSE? STOP BY NATURE'S TREASURE CHEST IN SPACES A ONE TROUGH FOUR TO SEE THE BEST SELECTION OF DESERT ROSES AND OTHER FINE MINERALS IN THE ENTIRE VALLEY. THAT'S SPACES A ONE THROUGH FOUR, JUST EAST OF THE MAIN SNACK BAR, FOR DESERT ROSES AND OTHER FINE GEMSTONES AND MINERALS.

The ad may have been corny and repetitious, but it got people's attention. Within minutes after its first airing, ladies were walking up to our tables and saying, "So that's a desert rose," or, "You didn't have these last year." Even more important, they bought them by the dozens. By the end of the season, we had sold nearly 4,000 of them.

When I compared inventory sheets at the end of our third season, the nickel and dime table had accounted for 37 percent of our total sales that winter. No wonder we had to hire a helper and give her a special inventory sheet for just nickel and dime! Sales of the souvenir-grade Indian art had dropped almost exactly in half, but overall sales increased 36 percent over our second season and 15 percent over the first. Diversification had definitely paid off, as we only knew one other vendor whose sales had increased that winter.

The second season we had a nickel and dime setup, its sales actually increased. This is understandable due to the wide variety of new items we added to the old stand-bys. In other words, we diversified within a given area rather than expanding into an entirely new one.

Nickel and dime sales dropped off drastically the third season, for several reasons. The third year blahs was only one of them. Most important, several other vendors copied us and began selling the same nickel and dime items we carried. We also lost our helper who had worked the nickel and dime table for two years. When she became ill midway through the season, we were forced to hire whatever help we could get on short notice. Two indifferent teenagers just don't equal one good person, teenager or adult, who is truly interested in what they sell.

The fourth season, nickel and dime sales dropped even further, but we still had our most successful season ever. By then, we recognized the need to diversify *every* year, so had already anticipated the additional decline. "You didn't have these last year" has become firmly established as our motto for the start of a new season. We also try to add something new at the end of each season, for a couple of reasons. First, it gives the season a good last minute sales boost. Second, it lets customers know there will be some new items in our display when they return the following winter.

Last winter, we broke away from our normal policy of diversification within our established merchandise base and went into a different field entirely. It proved to be our most successful change of all. Most important, it is built-in insulation against the third year blahs due to its very nature. It is, quite simply, a natural to keep customers coming back for more, year after year.

A couple of years ago, we began buying used paperbacks at our summer markets and using them to trade or sell outright to the local used book store. Finally, we decided to sell them ourselves at the swap meet. "The same people sell used books there year after year, so they must make money at it," my wife said.

We were in a unique position to take advantage of our situation. Normally, we work a summer market where there is little demand for used books, either paperback or hardcover. Due to this, it's possible to buy good used paperbacks for practically nothing.

In our winter market, the opposite situation exists. Most of the customers are retirees who like to read. They will pay premium prices for books by well-known and popular authors. The diversity of supply and demand between the two markets allows us to make a good profit and still sell our books at a competitive price.

My wife is a former librarian while I spent nearly 20 years working in the printing and publishing industries. She reads romances and science fiction while I like Westerns, true war and mysteries. Our new helper reads horror novels and true crime. Collectively, the three of us are well-informed on most of the categories we carry, although none of us is an expert in all.

Since our setup is located on the bottom row next to the parking lot, we're the first book dealer customers see. We're also the only one located under a canopy. This prevents the book covers from becoming sun-faded. It also allows customers to browse comfortably in an area partially shielded from the usual hustle and bustle of a busy swap meet.

While many dealers group their books strictly according to price, we arrange ours by category and even by author (the Louis Lamour box sells out entirely *early* in the season). With the books arranged by category, a customer can find the author and title he or she wants without searching through a lot of irrelevant material. We also sell only books in good condition, and clean the cover of each one. More than one customer has commented they thought our books were new. We also do book searches for customers, charging an extra quarter on top of the selling price for our service. Sometimes we can find what a customer wants, sometimes not, but we at least try. That alone keeps them coming back.

Our original intention was for the book setup to be a temporary thing, generating income early in the season when the demand for our Indian and Southwestern items is lowest. Unfortunately, things didn't work out as planned. Due to the overall poor economy, sales of our regular merchandise last year never did reach anticipated levels. Book sales far exceeded our expectations, however, and by early spring we were being run ragged just trying to maintain a decent inventory. We discovered new sources for used paperbacks out of sheer necessity and had good sales right up until the last day of the season. We had hoped the books would be an "in addition to" and would increase our sales. They were actually an "instead of." But at least we had an "instead of," which was more than a lot of other vendors had. Many reported their sales were down a third from the preceding winter.

At this writing, the true start of our winter season is still several weeks away. We are, however, already selling at our winter market. We're only putting a few pieces of Indian art on display, but have increased the space devoted to the book setup by almost 50 percent. They're selling even better than last year. Thanks to books alone, we've just had our best October ever, and without the expense of traveling away from home to do it.

Despite the present emphasis on books, we've already added several new lines to our Indian and Southwestern inventory in hopes of increasing sales in that area once the season really gets rolling. We've also increased the paperback inventory to almost double what we started with last year. That way, we're prepared for whichever way sales go this winter. If both categories show a significant increase, we'll be extremely happy. But one thing is certain. As long as we can continue to stock the authors and titles that are in demand, there isn't much danger of the book setup falling victim to the third year blahs.

There are, of course, numerous other factors which can cause a reduction in sales and create a need to diversify. Chief among these are:

1. *Monkey See, Monkey Do.* If you're successful at selling something that is readily available, it won't be long before your competitors will begin selling the same thing. This is especially true of swap meets. Too much competition kills a market for everyone. When too many other monkeys copy this monkey, this monkey will go out and find another banana tree.

2. *Poor Economy.* There are only two things that sell really well when times are tough: luxury items and basic necessities. This may sound contradictory, but it's true. While the Big Three auto makers post record losses, there is still a waiting list to buy a Lamborghini.

3. *Inclement Weather.* Virtually every shadow merchant who works outdoors is subject to the whims of Mother Nature. There is nothing you can do about it except protect yourself and merchandise as best you can and try to weather the storm (pun intended).

4. *The Fad Is Over.* Various fad items *can* sell well for a limited time, but timing is all-important. Several years ago, a certain exercise machine was being advertised on TV for $19.95, plus shipping and handling. Within a few weeks, a cheap Taiwan imitation was being sold at swap meets throughout the country. One fellow we know sold every one he had in just one weekend for $10. He didn't restock them, which was a smart move. A couple of weeks later, at least a half dozen other vendors were selling them. The price suddenly dropped to $4. Within a few weeks, one fellow was trying to dispose of his remaining stock at $2 each.

5. *Wholesale Cost Prices An Item Out Of The Market.* This has happened to a couple of items we carried. In one case, the wholesale cost rose almost 50 percent in less than two

years. Customers quit buying after we raised our price 20 percent. Needless to say, we quickly dropped that item as it was impossible to get a keystone on it at that point.

6. *Overall Change In Buying Patterns.* The change may be seasonal, as in Christmas decorations or summer beach-wear, or it may be gradual and harder to predict. Long-term changes often take place over a number of years. Long-playing records were popular for at least two generations, but slowly gave way to compact discs. Once the trend started, it snowballed. Try to anticipate such changes to the best of your ability and be ready to swing your inventory in whatever direction a trend indicates.

7. *Lack Of Availability.* Manufacturers can go out of business or drop a certain item due to poor overall sales. This can come as a shock if your sales of that item are generally good. At the other extreme, the manufacturer may be only temporarily behind on production due to an overwhelming demand or a shortage of raw materials. Any of the above possibilities are sufficient reason to be very cautious about dealing with only one product or supplier. It helps to have a backup source or two.

Several years ago, the owner of a small company we dealt with was killed in an auto accident. Despite the presence of several employees, it was basically a one-man operation. We had to find new sources for several items *fast*. Fortunately, we were able to locate alternate sources for everything except one item within a month's time. We simply dropped that one item from our inventory.

No matter how good sales may be at present, remember that diversification will be necessary at some point. This is true even when selling something that is in demand year after year, as there will invariably be a slump in sales at some point. With this in mind I have some final hints for diversification:

1. *Find something that complements your present line rather than making a complete change.* Of course, if sales drop drastically, it may be necessary to phase out the present line and switch to a new one entirely. However, merely adding complementary items often increases the sales of older ones. As an example, we branched out from just Indian art to include Indian artifacts and Southwestern decorator items. Now customers often say, "I could decorate my whole house from this one booth." In fact, one lady did buy enough recently to decorate an entire room. She bought a Navajo rug, a couple of limited edition sculptures, a wall hanging, a Southwest decor basket and several other items. As far as I know, ours was the only booth she patronized at that particular show. Another lady bought a one-of-a-kind piece of pottery and wound up repainting her living room to complement it.

2. *Keep an accurate inventory sheet to chart trends.* As I explained earlier, this practice enabled me to determine exactly where our sales declined or increased during our second winter season. It also clearly indicated that the situation would only worsen if we didn't make some drastic changes the following winter. Also, it can sometimes tell you a certain item or type of merchandise is actually selling better than you thought. When working a variety of markets, an inventory sheet can also show what sells in a given area. This summer, we worked four different shows within a 20-mile radius of each other. Theoretically, the crowd should have been roughly the same type of people at each show. However, one of our best selling items sold very poorly at one show, but set all-time records at the other three. Next year, we will know not to bother taking that item to the one show, but will increase our inventory for the other three. Keeping track of each and every sale is a lot of work, and may be downright impossible when selling a lot of small

items on a particularly busy day. In that case, just do the best you can. In the long run those inventory sheets may well spell the difference between success and failure.

3. *Don't become an inventory junkie.* Doubling the size of a small inventory will usually increase sales by a significant amount. Doubling one that is already large may not increase sales sufficiently to warrant the investment. It's especially easy to fall into the trap when diversifying. A new item may sell well at first, but sales could rapidly decline due to any number of factors. When this happens, you may have a fairly large inventory of slow-moving stock, yet be short on other items that you *know* would sell better if you had increased the inventory in those areas.

   Even though it hurts to do so, reduce the price on slow-moving items to clear out the inventory. If necessary, reduce the sale price to below your wholesale cost. It's far better to sell out at a loss and reinvest the proceeds in something that will sell than to sit on merchandise that is obviously a dud, hoping to eventually get top dollar for it. Remember, a business is supposed to support you, not the other way around. A large inventory that isn't selling doesn't put any money in your pocket. Where is the fine line between adequate inventory expansion and becoming an inventory junkie? *Everyone* in the business would like to know the answer to that one.

4. *Above all, try something different if sales are down.* If you can't possibly afford to diversify, that's when it's most important to do it! If it's totally out of the question for one reason or another, at least rearrange your display so it looks different. This alone will sometimes increase sales of otherwise slow-moving items. Customers may not notice something in the back of the display, but they will notice it on the front table. We recently changed the arrangement of our paperback setup, shifting a couple of slow-moving

categories to the very front of the display. Sales in those categories increased, yet there was no decline in the sales of the categories that had previously occupied that position. People who wanted ladies' romances and major novels already knew we had them, while science fiction and mystery fans discovered we had something for them, also.

Other People, Other Units

At some point, it's only natural for a growth-oriented, reasonably successful shadow merchant to consider expanding into other units. This is especially true for one who is new at the game and is making a profit, but not doing as well as he or she would like. It's easy to say, "If I'm making $300 per week now,

two units would give me $600, three would give me $900, etc."
A good basic idea on the surface, but what works for large
chains of retail stores doesn't necessarily work for shadow
merchants.

Based on personal experience, I have a very hard-nosed attitude on the subject. My advice on other units is: DON'T DO IT!

This statement is, however, overly simplistic. I know some
shadow merchants who are firmly convinced a second unit or
multiple ones are profitable. "If I have a slow day, my wife's
(son's, daughter's, etc.) unit usually makes up the difference,"
they say. Think about that for a minute. What they are actually
saying is that it takes two units to ensure consistently good day-
to-day sales. With the right winning combination described
earlier, one unit should be sufficient, at least most of the time.

Second or multiple units *can* be profitable, provided the
following factors are present:

1. There is a sufficient markup on the merchandise to ensure
    an adequate profit after paying salaries or commissions,
    space rent, etc. Don't overlook "hidden" costs. These can
    include special packaging for the customer, printed litera-
    ture describing the product, advertising, sales tax and credit
    card charges if included in the price, shipping from or travel
    costs to suppliers, etc.

2. Merchandise preparation for the other unit(s) requires a
    minimum of time and energy on your part. (Basically, if it
    involves anything more than pricing each item and prepar-
    ing an inventory list, forget it. We've found there is always
    someone wanting a slice of the pie if you're successful, but
    no one willing to help make the pie.)

3. You are assured a steady supply of enough merchandise to
    adequately stock two or more units. (Don't short-change
    yourself just to supply someone else. Whether you realize it
    or not, *it costs you more to operate their unit than your
    own*.)

4. The other unit sells *only* your merchandise, and not several other people's as well. (Those running it will naturally put the most effort into selling what makes the most money for them. If it isn't your merchandise, tough luck.)
5. You can initially supply another unit from extra inventory on hand, which is already paid for. Under no circumstances should you *ever* go into debt to supply someone else. If they don't produce, it's your head that's on the chopping block, not theirs.)
6. The people running other units have a proven track record of success as shadow merchants, or at least show excellent potential. (Some have been in the business for years, but are still living from hand to mouth. They say all they need is that big break. Avoid such losers like the plague. They already have a proven record of failure, and won't succeed even if you hand them that big break.)
7. There is sufficient demand for your product in the market area so a second unit won't actually be competing with yours. (There is enough competition in business without wasting your time, energy and money creating more for yourself. If there isn't any competition, keep it that way.)

If even one of the above factors is missing, a second unit stands a good chance of being more trouble than it's worth. If two or more are missing, disastrous results are virtually guaranteed. Precisely why is best illustrated by what happened to us during our first and second years in the business.

Toward the end of our first winter season, another couple who worked the same swap meet decided to visit friends at another swap meet halfway across the state. Naturally, they planned to sell there for the two weekends they would be gone. "Tom and Lois sell the same thing as their friends, and don't want to compete with them," my wife informed me after visiting with Lois one day. "They want to know if they can take some of our merchandise with them to sell on commission. I told Lois we'd pay them 25 percent of whatever they sell, plus space rent."

"That's too much," I replied, "We don't make anything on a deal like that."

"If we offered them any less, it wouldn't be enough to make it worthwhile for them," she countered.

I was still opposed to the idea, but reluctantly agreed since we were already committed. After all, we had enough duplicate inventory that we could supply them without hurting our own sales potential. At least it would give us a chance to see if the concept of a second unit might work for us.

Lois had been honest enough to tell us not to expect any miracles, so we were ecstatic when she called the following Sunday night. "We sold over $800 worth and need restocking for next weekend," she said. "I'll put a check in the mail for what we sold first thing tomorrow morning."

On the surface, it looked like their sales had been profitable for both of us. The retail price of the merchandise was based on a keystone, so replacement cost was $400. With $200 out for their commission, we theoretically also made $200, less $16 for space rent, for a net profit of $184. But when *all* factors were figured in, it was actually quite a bit less. The actual costs that were immediately calculable were as follows:

Factor	Cost	Theoretical Net
Wholesale Replacement	$400	$400
Commission	$200	$200
Space Rent	$ 16	$184
Sales Tax (at 7.5%)	$ 60	$124
Credit Card Charges	$ 9	$113

The final theoretical net would still appear to yield a net profit of 14 percent, which is marginally acceptable. However, expenses which are not immediately calculable, or which are incalculable, reduce it still more. Chief among these is travel cost for the 400-mile round trip each week to replace merchandise. At the time, we estimated it to be $100 per trip, including gas, a meal out and normal wear and tear on our pickup. If the second unit made 40 percent of the total sales of both units for a given weekend, it should bear 40 percent of the $100 travel expense. That would be another $40 deducted from our theoretical profit. Out of what was left, there were other minor costs such as collect phone calls from Lois on Sunday night to report sales, brochures describing the merchandise, packaging, etc.

Unfortunately, we were new in the business and too naive (and busy) to calculate all of the above factors. If we had known then what we know now, we never would have tried a second unit for more than a couple of weekends. Instead, we made a natural mistake and saw only the potential for extra sales and our alleged immediate profit rather than the bottom line.

The real gremlins in our arrangement were the percentage of commission and the space rent. Remember, a weekend when they grossed $800 yielded us a *theoretical* profit of $113. That was far more than our actual profit. Using the same basic percentages and an equal amount for space rent, a $300 gross would only have yielded a theoretical net profit of $33.12, or 11 percent. A really bad weekend with only $100 gross would yield a theoretical profit of 37 cents, for an actual loss when all other costs are figured in.

With a 20 percent commission structure and them paying their own space rent, we would have made a theoretical net profit of $171, or 21 percent. That percentage would have remained constant, no matter what the gross. Of course, on a $100 gross weekend we would have still lost money, but not nearly as much.

Tom and Lois worked hard for us, and we soon began re-
ferring to them as the Terrific Twins. That started out to be a
temporary arrangement for a couple of weekends wound up
lasting well over a year. It finally ended when Lois became ill
and it appeared she would require lengthy hospitalization.
During that first summer, there were periods when their
gross sales exceeded ours. They had some retirement income,
but realized we depended entirely on our shadow merchant receipts for a living. More often than not, they would send us
their entire gross receipts for a summer weekend. "We'll settle
up on our commission and space rent this winter, when things
are easier for you," Lois would say.

People who demonstrate that kind of consideration and
loyalty deserve a response in kind. Since we were well stocked
with merchandise, we often sent them far more than they asked
for. We knew they could probably sell it faster than we could.
We were right. At one point, they were working a swap meet
which was busiest on Wednesdays, a day when most other swap
meets are closed. Lois called us on her lunch break one day to
tell us she had just sold her entire inventory of our best artist's
work. We had a refill package on its way to her in just a couple
of hours.

As we entered our second winter season, my wife still be-
lieved we could make more money if we ran two units at the
swap meet. I wasn't convinced, but didn't have a Plan B that
was any better, so went along with her idea. This proved to be
unfortunate, for that was the winter of the Neanderthal Twins.

We had offered the second unit to Tom and Lois, but they
wanted to work in another state, so they introduced us to the
Neanderthal Twins. I wasn't particularly impressed with them,
but reserved judgment until later. After all, my initial impression of Tom and Lois had been wrong. I was also wrong about
the Neanderthal Twins, but in the opposite direction. If anything, they fell far short of the level of mediocrity I had ex-

pected. I could write an entire book about the frustrations of a winter spent working with them, but will reduce it to a few sentences.

The economy was bad that winter and everyone's sales were down from the previous year. At the time, we considered ourselves lucky to have two units operating. That was a bad mistake. The gross for both units was a little higher than our own for the previous winter, but our actual profit was less. Virtually all the profits from the Neanderthal Twins' unit as well as some of the profit from ours, went back into more inventory for them. In retrospect, all we were doing was working like dogs to hand them the means of taking sales away from us, and paying them 25 percent commission plus space rent to do it.

We thought the profit situation might improve once they went to their summer location in another state. It actually got worse. Many weekends their space rent exceeded gross sales. Their main summer market was located near four military installations. They always managed to be somewhere else on military payday weekends, when sales there would have been best. Some weekends they were working, others they were off visiting relatives or fishing.

Sales at our own summer market were mediocre at best, but we grossed more in one particularly good day there than they did in over three months. We were literally losing money on every item they sold, but Mrs. Neanderthal would still call up and say, "We need more merchandise." She well knew we had stripped our own unit badly to supply them, but that didn't matter. It was still, "We need more merchandise."

In addition to supplying the Neanderthal Twins for the summer, we also got involved in an Indian show in Germany. That little adventure proved even more disastrous. In both cases, it had been impossible to adequately stock them from inventory on hand. We had always done business on a cash basis, but bought on credit for the Neanderthal Twins and the German fiasco. When the payments came due, there was no money to make them. It's no fun explaining to irate suppliers that you can't pay them when you promised simply because you counted on incompetents who let you down. At that point, it was obvious we had made a very bad mistake going out on a limb to supply other people, then expecting them to perform. We had over $15,000 worth of merchandise in their hands, and very little in our own. That mistake almost cost us everything we had.

It's impossible to calculate our total losses for that summer. We estimate our actual, out-of-pocket losses at roughly $10,000. We had to make that up by working extra hard the next few years just to pay off debts that never would have existed if we hadn't counted on other people. Our overall losses in terms of credit, credibility and potential earnings for our own unit will never be known.

As I said at the beginning of this chapter, I now have an extremely hard-nosed attitude regarding other units. It can be narrowed down to: With few exceptions, those who have what it takes to make it as shadow merchants are already doing it on their own. Those who don't have it simply won't make it even if you hand them success on a silver platter. Don't waste your time, energy and money being a baby sitter to them.

Other units might work for some people, but they don't work for the Coopers. Those that are successful are usually family enterprises in which everyone has a stake in the ultimate success or failure of the business.

The winter of the Neanderthal Twins, our own unit had its worst selling season ever. The following year, we diversified as outlined in the preceding chapter. Our one unit grossed more than all three units combined the previous winter. We didn't work any harder, and we didn't have to pay anyone 25 percent commission plus space rent to do it!

Hire A Heather!

Believe it or not, I have some good news about teenagers. Not all of them are worthless zombies who are only interested in sex, drugs, wild parties and rock concerts. A surprising number are highly intelligent, industrious, well-groomed and courteous. There are even a few who could put Donald Trump to shame when it comes to hustling a buck.

Over the years, my wife and I have had the privilege of knowing and/or working with a number of teenagers who are shadow merchants themselves, or who work for one. Most were a real credit to the human race. A few were outstanding examples of what teenagers can achieve.

When I think of teenagers selling at swap meets, I always think of Heather first. She is the one person in this book who appears under her real name, an honor I feel she richly deserves. In her case, spell Heather s-u-c-c-e-s-s. When she was only thirteen, I complimented her mother for teaching her to be such an outstanding salesperson. "Are you kidding?" the mother replied. "I should take lessons from her!"

Of course, Heather owes her success to a couple of secrets she learned during her pre-teen years. These secrets won't benefit an adult directly, but they can help indirectly and I will reveal them shortly.

Like many regular vendors who sell used goods, Heather starts her selling day early. She makes the rounds of other vendors who are cleaning out their garage or attic. If she sees something that appeals to her, she will ask the selling price. If she thinks it's too high, she will go into her Academy Award performance. With a downcast expression on her cherubic face, she will turn her pocket inside out to reveal a single quarter. "A dollar, mister?" she will say. "I can't afford that much. All I've got is a quarter." Of course, the seller doesn't know about the roll of bills she has in her other pocket. More often than not Heather will walk away with the desired item at her price.

Secret Number One: One-time vendors often feel sorry for a cute kid who wants something, but who doesn't have the money to buy it. Remember, they're simply getting rid of unwanted items, not trying to make a living at selling. This approach seldom works on a pro selling new merchandise.

Upon returning to her own selling space with her purchases (usually stuffed animals), Heather will establish a selling price for each item and position it strategically on her table. When customers stop to examine her wares, she really turns on the charm. "Isn't that a nice bunny rabbit?" she says. "Look how clean it is. It's practically brand new, and I bet your little girl would just love to have it. It's so soft and cuddly. Don't you think it's worth two dollars?" Invariably, her table will be nearly empty by the time the selling session ends.

Secret Number Two: People love to buy from cute kids, especially those who show some initiative. They believe that ambitious teenagers are in the minority and want to encourage them by patronizing their stands.

Unfortunately, not everyone has a Heather in the family. This includes the Coopers. There are, however, plenty of teenagers in the world who are looking for part-time jobs and who are willing to work. Some of them even have the potential to become another Heather. We haven't been lucky enough to find her equal yet, but have had a couple of girls working for us who were real assets to the setup. They were about as opposite in physical appearance as two people could possibly be, but both were good workers of far above average intelligence. Being young, they sometimes goofed off when business was slow. That was perfectly understandable, as most people become easily bored under such circumstances.

CJ was short, dark, and the cutest thing since the teddy bear. She was too shy to be a very good salesperson, but was unbelievably good at setting up and tearing down. We only had to show her how to do something once, then she could do it quickly and correctly thereafter. She was one of those rare people who can, despite superior intelligence, maintain their concentration on the most mundane of tasks.

Willow was as tall as CJ was short, as fair as CJ was dark. If anything, she was actually much too intelligent for her own good. Her brain would often go into neutral during routine setup and teardown tasks. However, this tendency was more

than offset by her selling ability. Although her area of responsibility was mainly the nickel and dime section, she would occasionally have to wait on customers in the Indian area when
my wife and I were both busy. If we didn't watch her, we would
find her trying to sell in both areas at the same time, even when
it wasn't necessary. To this day, I swear if we had left her alone
for half an hour, she would have tried to sell *everything*, including the canopy and tables. Talk about a kid who understood
how commission sales work! If we could have just combined
the best qualities of CJ and Willow into one person, we would
have had a girl that was too good to be true.

Surprisingly, the person who showed the most potential for
developing into another Heather was a teenage boy. He hadn't
been with us very long when he started asking questions like,
"How much does your merchandise cost?" or "What does it cost
to rent a space here?" At first we were a bit evasive in our answers. However, as he asked more questions about the licensing
requirements, etc., we realized he wasn't just being nosey. We
could practically see the wheels turning in his brain as he considered the possibilities of starting his own swap meet business.

"You know, it's really tough trying to work at a grocery or
fast food place and go to school, too," he said one day. "They
want you to work evenings during the week, when you have
homework to do. But in a business like this, just on weekends,
a guy can have a part-time job and still keep his grades up."

Once he brought his train of thought out into the open, we
explained about keystones, tristones, overhead, etc. Since he
was considering starting out with used goods, we suggested he
visit yard sales and auctions to look for merchandise, a practice
common to regular used goods vendors.

Since he would be starting out in the summer, we advised
him not to try the winter market we were working. "Business is
good right now," we explained, "but everything will fall apart in
another month. Our sales will actually increase over the next

couple of weeks, as the snowbirds are getting ready to go home. The first of next month, there'll be a mass exodus of RVs like you wouldn't believe.

"For summer sales, try setting up at Broad Valley. They have a good crowd, even in the summer. It's actually a better market for used goods at anytime of the year. Most of the crowd is from low-income families."

We haven't seen the fellow since the winter season ended, so don't know if he decided to try his luck as a shadow merchant. If he did, he will definitely have to work on his selling technique, which was far from the best. However, he will have one advantage which should help offset this in the beginning. Like Heather, he thinks in terms of buying at the right price, then selling at a good profit. He realizes that without profits, businesses would cease to exist.

One last word on hiring teenagers: If you find a really good one, pay him or her as much as you would an adult, or at least nearly as much. It's possible to hire good people cheaply if they're truly desperate for work, but you won't keep them cheaply. It's actually to your advantage to pay them a decent wage, as they can increase sales more than enough to offset the cost.

An Officer And A Gentleman

By an act of Congress, a commissioned officer in the armed forces is "an officer and a gentleman." In today's military establishment, the term "an officer and a lady" would probably be appropriate for a female officer. Military officers are expected to look and act like ladies and gentlemen, and are trained to do so. Mere civilians receive no such training. Unfortunately, all too many clearly demonstrate that lack.

Several years ago, my wife and I were eating breakfast at the restaurant in one of our busiest national monuments. I looked at some of the other customers and was appalled at what I saw. "You know," I commented, "the American tourist has to be the biggest slob in the world... unless it's a swap meet vendor."

Basically, proper dress and conduct for any shadow merchant, including swap meet vendors, involves nothing more than using a little common sense.

No one in their right mind would expect a shadow merchant to dress like Fred Astaire or Ginger Rogers going out on the town. They work hard all day, under conditions that are less than ideal. Many have to set up and tear down large displays and are in constant danger of tearing or staining their clothing. Their desire to dress comfortably is understandable. However, being comfortable doesn't mean they can't also presentable.

There is nothing wrong with wearing a T-shirt and Levi's when selling in a casual atmosphere, as long as they are clean and reasonably new. The same applies to shorts and summer tops. The key word here is *conservative.*

We recently worked an art show where the opposite was demonstrated by another seller who could best be described as centerfold material. Each morning, the wives would do a slow burn as their husbands eagerly awaited the arrival of Scrumptious Suzie. One morning she was almost wearing a fringed bikini. Another day, it was a matching halter and shorter-than-short shorts set. Although she definitely had the shape for such outfits, she didn't have the sense to confine their use to the beach or poolside.

By contrast, our little CJ was every bit as attractive as Scrumptious Suzie, but in an entirely different way. It was obvious from both her dress and her conduct that CJ was a *lady.*

Whether inherited from her parents or a result of her upbringing I'm not sure, but she definitely had class with a capital "C."

Unfortunately, a certain percentage of shadow merchants have a lot of the wrong kind of class. It's all low. They also seem intent on proving just how low it is.

I've seen all too many sellers at swap meets sporting several days' growth of beard and dressed as if they were ready for a night on the town on Skid Row. Some had horrendously gross beer bellies hanging out below their T-shirts and a case of rancidius armpitus which would have been the envy of a Roman galley slave. You didn't dare stand downwind of them.

As if the above offenses weren't enough, some were guzzling beer as fast as they could pop the top off a can and were smoking cigars that smelled like burning rubber. Their typical sales approach might be something like: "Hey, lady! Come take a look at my #%@#* stuff. I got the best *#%@&#@ prices in this whole *#$@%#& area." Some of these people were actually selling, or trying to sell, top quality, new merchandise. They simply didn't realize that personal appearance and conduct can attract customers — or drive them away.

Men aren't the only offenders when it comes to dress and personal conduct. Some women feel more comfortable going braless, but should take a good look at themselves in the mirror before heading out for a day's selling. Ditto for those who wear shorts. There is nothing attractive about mammaries that sag below the waistline or flabby thighs laced with cellulite and varicose veins. The idea is to make customers reach for their wallets, not a barf bag.

By contrast, some female vendors dress attractively and comfortably and conduct themselves in a ladylike manner. At least two ladies at our winter location are prime examples. Teddy Bear and Buttercup always look neat and feminine, even when dressed casually. They are also busy selling all day — to women as well as men.

Some shadow merchants who present an otherwise favorable appearance have habits which may be offensive or at the very least irritating. They may pick their noses, spit tobacco juice, or pace back and forth when they aren't busy. Others may have regional speech patterns of which they are unaware, ending every sentence with an unnecessary word or phrase. Canadians are notorious for ending a sentence with "eh" while many Southerners add "y'hear?"

If you have a video camera, by all means tape yourself making an imaginary sales pitch. Have a friend pose as a customer, asking typical questions about your merchandise. Play the tape back and watch for any errors you might have made. Your first impression will probably inspire you to ask, "Do I look *that* bad to people?" Probably not. Remember, you are purposely being self-critical. *Do* make a sincere effort to correct any serious faults which might be offensive to customers. I know of at least one sales school that uses the videotaping technique with excellent results. Students can observe their mistakes and correct them *before* they have a chance to repeat them in the field.

In the final analysis, a shadow merchant should avoid offensive conduct and should dress in a manner which is comfortable, yet appropriate for the season and the type of merchandise he or she is selling. Remember, being a shadow merchant is a job, even if you are your own boss. Very few employers will tolerate an employee who swills beer all day, talks like a drunken sailor and dresses like a skid row bum. Customers tend to shy away from a shadow merchant who behaves in the same manner.

President Eisenhower didn't have an exclusive on being an officer and a gentleman. Princess Grace wasn't the only lady who ever lived. You may know someone who isn't rich or famous, yet is their equal in those categories. Aren't you lucky if that someone is you?

Rich People Have Dry Feet

After several years as a shadow merchant, I've come to an interesting conclusion. The main difference between rich people and shadow merchants is that rich people have dry feet. After all, they never get soaking wet trying to protect their merchandise when a sudden rainstorm hits. There are some former shadow merchants who are now rich, but I'll bet they got wet more than once before achieving their wealthy status.

Although its influence will vary from one part of the country to another, inclement weather *can* affect any area in which a shadow merchant is working. For this reason, many swap meets have indoor selling spaces, especially in the East and Pacific Northwest. There are some which are located entirely indoors, even in the sunny Southwest. Contrary to popular belief, that region does have a rainy season during the summer. This past summer, my wife and I had wet feet for two days straight, and drove home from an art show under threat of a hurricane alert. Needless to say, sales were poor.

Some experienced shadow merchants have developed an uncanny knack for predicting a sudden change in the weather, no matter what the official prediction is. This is especially true of swap meet and art show vendors who work outdoors. They will suddenly feel it's time to tear down, even if there are only a few clouds in the sky. Their neighbors may sit back and watch with amusement for awhile. A half hour later, after hearing a distant "ka-ba-ba-boom!" and seeing lightning on the horizon, they will be scrambling themselves.

Although very little can be done about the weather, there are a few precautions which can be taken, especially against rain. Sometimes a storm will last only a few minutes, or will break during the morning hours. If this occurs in a market where sales are best in the afternoon, a vendor could lose several hours' prime selling time by tearing down early. Many vendors work under canopies, which offer *some* protection against both sun and rain. They help, but aren't a perfect solution, especially if they have flat roofs. A cloudburst can dump several gallons of water on a flat roof. Gravity will force the water into the center, making it necessary to "bail" the canopy by pushing up from below. Canopies with peaked roofs are much better for water drainage. They also have more eye appeal since they are taller and seem more spacious.

Even when working under a canopy, some form of waterproof table cover is a good idea. Some vendors use plastic tarps, but we prefer long sheets of transparent or semi-transparent 6 mil plastic. It protects the merchandise just as well, yet still allows customers to see it. People will naturally head for shelter under the nearest canopy when the rain starts. Some of them will browse and buy while waiting for the storm to end. More than once, we've made a large sale from "under wraps" simply because a customer could still see the merchandise clearly.

Wind can be even more devastating than rain, as we learned the hard way last spring. We weathered the first flurry of rain easily. As it was already afternoon, we were tearing down when the freak windstorm hit. It was bad enough to be the featured item on the 10 o'clock news that night. I watched it in the hospital emergency room. My wife couldn't see it or anything else, as she had been hit in the eye by flying debris when our canopy blew over. The framework was big (over 800 square feet under roof), and heavy, being constructed of one-inch pipe. But it was no match for those winds. A second rainstorm followed, along with hail. By the time it was over, we had lost over $3,500 worth of merchandise. If we had been set up at a dirt market, the canopy never would have blown over as we could have staked it down. But, the owners of our winter market take a very dim view of people driving stakes through their asphalt.

Perhaps the worst combination of weather conditions, barring a tornado or hurricane, is a dust storm followed by a light rain shower. First everything gets a coat of dust, then rain-splattered. In the Southwest, this is known as a six-inch rain, meaning six inches between drops. The merchandise may not be ruined, but it will need a thorough cleaning to make it saleable. It's usually possible to see a dust storm coming a few minutes in advance. This gives you a chance to cover your display and secure the covers against the wind. Also be sure to pick up any empty boxes and put them away, otherwise you may still be looking for them a week later. Once all is secure, about the only thing you can do is get under cover yourself and wait out the storm. Dust storms followed by rain usually don't last long, although there can be exceptions.

Just about any type of merchandise or display fixture which can be damaged by rain should also be protected from fog. This is sometimes easier said than done, as fog can creep under a canopy where rain doesn't reach unless windblown. Fog usually burns off by mid-morning in our area, but may linger in seacoast areas. About all you can do is wait it out.

Even areas which are noted for mild winters occasionally have extreme cold spells. Believe it or not, it can even snow in the Sun Belt. If you arrive at your selling location and find it is snowing, about the safest course of action is to go back home. Just write the day off as a lost cause and either go back to bed or curl up in front of the fireplace with a good book. Customers probably won't be out in that kind of weather, so why risk catching a cold or pneumonia?

If the weather is merely cold, but the sun is shining, go ahead and set up. You can keep warm by taking a large thermos of coffee, tea or hot chocolate to work and by dressing in layers. I usually start out on cold mornings with a thermal undershirt, flannel shirt, fleece-lined vest, sweater, Levi jacket and sheepskin jacket. My wife will usually wear a wool sweater over a turtleneck, with her down-filled parka on top. As the temperature rises, we shed the outer layers until we are usually down to shirtsleeves in the afternoon. As evening approaches and the temperature drops, we reverse the process.

In the summer, we carry plenty of ice water, iced tea and cold pop with us to ward off dehydration. If electricity is available, we also plug in a small fan; it will stir the air just enough to create an illusion of coolness. We often work a particular swap meet in the summer that has both day and night selling sessions. A surprising number of people come out after the sun goes down. Once you're acclimated to the heat, 100-degree temperatures are perfectly bearable if the sun is down and there is a light breeze.

We've learned that it's a good policy to have clothing for both warm and cool weather with us when traveling, no matter what the time of year. Boston can have a heat wave in February, or a cool spell can strike the desert Southwest in July. The weather can also vary greatly from one day to the next. A couple of years ago, we literally had icicles hanging from the side mirror of our pickup on Monday, and were driving around in shirtsleeves with the windows open on Tuesday. Talk about quick changes!

After working in a particular area for awhile, you should be able to judge what the weather will be for the next few hours with some degree of accuracy. You won't be infallible, but should be right most of the time. When trying to decide whether or not to work on any "iffy" day, an FM weather radio can be a godsend. Most large metropolitan areas have a US Weather Bureau office near the airport. They broadcast the weather around the clock on one of three different FM frequencies, with hourly updates. Listening to the weather radio several times during the selling day has saved our bacon more than once. Sometimes our neighbors at the winter location wonder why we're tearing down when the sun is shining and the wind is calm. All I have to do is yell, "Hailstorm with 45 mph winds over Black Mountain, headed this way." That wakes them up in a hurry!

Part Two:

Types of Markets

Swap Meets And Flea Markets

Swap meets and flea markets are an outgrowth of village market days which are probably as old as civilization itself. No one knows just when or where the first one was started in the United States. Some have been operating continuously since the

1930s. At least one in rural Kentucky can trace its roots back to the 1800s.

Originally, swap meets and flea markets were small, open-air markets where people could buy, sell and trade used goods. They have since developed into *big* business, with many of the larger ones catering to vendors of new merchandise. Indoor markets are commonplace in sections of the country where inclement weather can be expected at any time of the year. In the Southwest, which is famous for its mild winter climate, outdoor swap meets prevail.

Some markets are small, one-day-a-week affairs held in vacant lots. At the other extreme, some are so large they run a shuttle service between the parking lot and selling area. I once told the owner of one large market that it reminded me of a cross between a miniature golf course, carnival, gypsy camp and Mexican border town. She laughed and said I had described it perfectly. Strange combination that it is, the place has its own weird charm that grows on you after awhile.

With literally thousands of them throughout the country, the local swap meet is a logical starting place for a beginning shadow merchant. There are several reasons for this:

- Many have been established for years and draw large crowds each weekend. These people comprise an already established customer base.
- Most swap meet customers have grown complacent at the sight of the same old vendors selling the same old thing every weekend, year after year. They will immediately notice a "new look" amidst row after row of look-alike stalls.
- It generally requires a much smaller investment to try working swap meets as opposed to other potential locations. As mentioned previously, my wife and I started with an initial investment of $43.75, plus $6 for space rent. We showed a profit the very first day. Of course, not everyone is lucky enough to start that small. A friend of ours was a

real high roller when he started. He had $62 invested in his initial setup! He now runs a total of three units in the two largest swap meets in the state, plus a very lucrative wholesale business. His combined operations consume an average of 15,000 packing boxes *per month*! Every penny he has invested in his business grew out of the profits from that initial $62 investment. Such growth in just eight years may seem phenomenal, and it isn't typical. But it *can* be duplicated by anyone who is reasonably intelligent and willing to work hard.

- It's possible to "get your feet wet" as a shadow merchant without investing in any merchandise at all. Simply clean out your garage, attic, closets or storage room. Haul the items you no longer want or need to the local swap meet this coming weekend. You can turn these discards into cash in your pocket while doing some reconnaissance. Observe the type of people who attend and what they buy. Are they low-income families with small children, looking for low-priced necessities? Are they mainly tourists who want regional souvenirs? Is the crowd a fairly even mixture of several types of customers? The answers to these questions can serve as a basis for deciding what type of new merchandise to sell. (Reread "The Winning Combination" and "Sell What You Like" before making a final decision.)

- In large metropolitan areas, there could well be more than a dozen swap meets within a 20 to 50 mile radius. This increases your possibilities for finding the right market for you. Even if the physical layout is identical, no two swap meets are exactly alike. Some are very good for one type of merchandise, quite poor for another. If you try several and don't like any of them, it's time to look for a different marketing approach or location.

There are, of course, also disadvantages to working swap meets as opposed to other locations. These include, but aren't necessarily limited to:

- Customers expect all prices to be negotiable. They usually are with a vendor who is cleaning out his garage. Some pros will negotiate on new merchandise, but most won't. Those who do are fools if they sell it too low a price just to make a sale. They aren't doing themselves or their fellow vendors any favors. Our policy is to negotiate *only* if an item is a slow seller or if the customer is inquiring about a price break on multiple purchases. The customer's attitude is also a key factor. We immediately resist someone who says, "I'll give you (amount)." We *will* consider negotiating on certain items if they say, "Could you possibly take any less?" or "Is that the lowest you'll go?" Even if we refuse the request, we will do so in a courteous manner.

- Competition can be fierce. At some larger swap meets, there may be several dozen vendors selling the same type of merchandise. This doesn't mean they're doing well with it. Usually they're just too lazy or stupid to find something that will sell and for which there is no competition. In such a situation, cutthroat pricing usually results, with no one making a decent profit. The worst offenders often display signs saying, "50% Off To Everyone," "Wholesale To The Public," or "Lower Than Discount." Avoid such shoddy merchandising practices, which some vendors resort to only in self-defense. Instead, look for that unusual item no one else sells, but which will have a wide appeal for your main customer base. If that item is your own creation and you can keep the process a secret, "monkey see, monkey do" may *never* apply!

- Many vendors are retirees who don't actually need to make a profit. They just want something to do with their time and enjoy meeting people. They may pay $1 wholesale for something and sell it for $1.10. There is simply no way a person who is trying to make a living can compete with them. (Again, look for that unusual item no one sells, but which has a wide appeal.)

- A lot of so-called customers are what I call "touchy-feelies." They may be well-mannered elsewhere, but have to touch and feel every item at the swap meet, with no intention of buying anything. The more expensive and fragile an item is, the more they have to act like a retarded baboon when handling it. Other people may not touch anything, but allow their children to run wild and touch and feel everything in sight. These kids may have anything from peanut butter to orange slush on their fingers, but the parents are usually too busy swilling beer to discipline them. (You can usually tell when someone is seriously interested in an expensive item. They will inspect it from every angle and discuss it in detail, but will seldom touch it until after they have actually purchased it.)

- Inclement weather can affect sales. This is true of *any* outdoor location, not just swap meets. Generally, we've found customers at our winter location don't buy if the temperature is below 65 degrees or above 85. Certain weekends are exceptions, especially when the snowbirds are getting ready to return home for the summer. On the Sunday before March 15th, they will come out in droves, even if the temperature is 40 degrees and there are 30 mph winds. They become *very* indignant when they discover most vendors had the good sense to stay home. Of course, *no one* will be out shopping in severe weather conditions such as a thunderstorm or blizzard.

- Some swap meets are highly seasonal. Business may be excellent during the summer and very poor in the winter, or vice versa. Reread the description of our winter market in

"The Winning Combination" for the best example of a seasonal market I can possibly give.

A more complete guide to working swap meets can be found in my first book, *How To Make Cash Money Selling At Swap Meets, Flea Markets, Etc.* (Loompanics Unlimited, 1988). Although it's geared specifically to those markets, there are some valuable tips in it for any type of shadow merchant venture.

Most larger swap meets and flea markets are listed in the Yellow Pages. To find those outside your immediate area, I recommend you consult the following publications:

The Official Directory To U.S. Flea Markets, House Of Collectibles, 201 East 50th Street, New York, New York 10022. Distributed by Ballantine Books, this handy little volume is now in its third edition. It can be found in better bookstores nationwide, or they can order it for you. Completely updated, it lists mainly those markets which are best for antiques and collectibles. The listings are *very* complete, even including space sizes and current rental fees.

West Coast Merchandiser, Sumner Publications, 72 North Street, Suite 201, Danbury, Connecticut 06810-5674. This monthly publication is distributed free at many of the better swap meets throughout the West, or is available by subscription. It contains a number of ads from some of the largest wholesale swap meet suppliers, plus a good selection of columns and articles of interest to the trade. Especially outstanding are the monthly "Editor's Column" by Alan Sanderson and articles by Earl Rishell. *Read them!* The swap meets listed at the back of *WCM* are only the ones where you can find the magazine, but they're a good starting point. Sister publications are *East Coast Merchandiser* and *Midwest Merchandiser,* which are available in those regions. Sumner also publishes an annual guide to *active* swap meets and flea markets. I've never seen a copy, but if they publish it, it's probably good.

There are, or at least used to be, two or three other swap meet guides. I can't recommend them as they seldom updated their listings, with one still listing a swap meet that has been out of business since the 1970s. There is simply *no* guide that lists every swap meet or flea market in the country. Many are so small as to be virtually unknown outside their immediate area. But, that doesn't necessarily mean they can't be lucrative. The first swap meet where my wife and I sold off our excess household goods was literally located in the parking lot of a country crossroads bar. It wasn't unusual to see a cow walking down the aisles. The handful of vendors there were all making money!

Most shadow merchants who have been working swap meets and flea markets for a number of years agree they aren't nearly as lucrative as they used to be. Vendors have to carry a larger inventory and work harder just to try to make the same money they did a few years ago. There are a number of reasons for this, not the least of which is the state of the economy.

Fortunately, these markets aren't the only option open to shadow merchants, but they are still a very good place to start. They allow you to "get your feet wet" in retailing before trying other, more difficult possibilities.

Street Corners

RETAIL SPACE AVAILABLE. High visibil-
ity, low, low rent. Call 123-4567
eves.

A classified ad like the above would be sure to elicit dozens
of telephone calls from potential lessees. Their initial interest

would quickly wane once they learned the retail spot wasn't a storefront at all, but a vacant lot! After all, who in their right mind would want to sell on a street corner or vacant lot?

No one — except some of the brightest and most successful shadow merchants in the business. One fellow I know works a combination of swap meets, fairs and street corners, depending on the time of year. He definitely prefers street corners to the other two. He says the customers are nicer and are more likely to buy and the rents are lower. As an example, he normally pays $25 per month to rent a street corner. The highest he has ever paid, for a *prime* spot in the parking lot of a large furniture store, was $15 per day.

Almost any fair-sized city will have several locations that are potentially good. If the local economy is even slightly depressed, there will be a number of choice spots just waiting for an enterprising shadow merchant. Look for a location that is highly visible on a main roadway, with easy access from and back onto the road. A defunct gas station or convenience market is almost ideal. Bear in mind that traffic flow will vary from day to day. A main thoroughfare in a commercial or industrial area that carries a lot of traffic on weekdays may have light traffic on weekends.

Of course, the first step is to check city ordinances to determine the legality of street vending. Some cities prohibit it altogether while others allow it as long as the street vendors abide by certain rules and regulations. One city with which I am familiar allows nothing on the ground but four wheels and two feet. In other words, no canopies or merchandise displayed on the ground. Another permits canopies, but they must be set at least 30 feet back from the roadway. The local police department can probably tell you whether or not street vending is legal in your city. If the desk sergeant doesn't know, he can refer you to the proper city office, which may be planning and zoning or the license bureau.

Have a list of potential locations handy in case you are asked where you want to set up. One spot might be zoned for commercial use while another is residential. Sales would be prohibited in the latter, except door-to-door. You will undoubtedly have to buy a city license. This will cost anywhere from a few dollars to several hundred, depending on the greed of the local bureaucracy.

Naturally, you will need to have permission from the property owner, but that's often easy to obtain. Some may want a ridiculously high rent, in which case you can forget them. Another may be more than happy to rent you his or her empty street corner or vacant lot for just enough money to pay the property tax. To find out who owns a particular parcel of land, simply visit the city or county recorder's or assessor's office. They will give you the information, which is a matter of public record.

Just about anything can be sold on street corners, but some items will sell better than others. Large items which are instantly recognizable from a distance are best. No one is going to pull off the road just to see what you have in the little bitty packages on a flat table. Some items which are generally, and profitably, sold on street corners in our area of the country include:

Car Dash and Seat Covers
Velvet Paintings
Brass Furniture and Accessories
Framed Prints
Stuffed Animals (the larger the better)
Lawn Furniture and Ornaments
Alpaca Rugs and Wall Hangings
Produce
Kites (Don't laugh! I know one fellow who does extremely well with kites, with some models fetching $160 each.)

Pumpkins and Christmas Trees (In season, with the same vendors usually selling them on the same location year after year.)

Recently my wife and I visited what has to be the ultimate street corner set-up. It was next to McDonald's in a small town near a busy winter resort area. Viewed from the road, the only merchandise which could be specifically identified were some ladies' two-piece outfits. However, the very size of the setup invited you to stop and browse. Inside her 4,000 square foot canopy, the owner had managed to cram just about everything imaginable, from Taiwan toys, makeup kits and cheap earrings to framed laser prints and hanging flower pot holders made from seashells. She informed us that it takes her and her husband a solid week to erect the canopy and arrange the merchandise displays. Since they sit in the same location seven days a week throughout the winter months and just close it up at night, that amount of work isn't excessive. While it would be nice to have such a setup, it definitely isn't for everyone. Many shadow merchants manage to make a living with a street corner setup which can be erected and torn down in just a few minutes each day.

One variation of street corner sales which has become increasingly prevalent in recent years is pushcarts, or one of the modern variations thereof. These tiny retail outlets on wheels had their origins in New York City's predominantly Jewish Lower East Side around the turn of the century. Up until the late 1800s, Jewish peddlers had managed to earn a living traveling through the hinterlands of the Eastern United States, selling everything from pots and pans to farm implements and dry goods. The founding of a then-small mail order firm called Montgomery Ward in 1872 began to render the farm-to-farm peddler's services obsolete. With the appearance of Sears, Roebuck & Co. in 1886, the more astute peddlers *really* saw the handwriting on the wall.

They took their carts to New York. Immigrants from Eastern Europe who couldn't find work copied them. They would cobble together a homemade cart, then push it through the city streets, selling everything from rags and bagels to chicken soup. By the early 1900s, there were 4,000 licensed pushcarts on the city's streets, the legal maximum, and an estimated 10,000 unlicensed ones. The city's police commissioner was more of a realist than a bureaucrat, once stating that the unlicensed carts' owners were only trying to make a living.

Today's pushcarts are a far cry from the originals. Most are commercially manufactured. Their owners may even haul them to their selling locations on specially constructed trailers. They are also far more lucrative than the originals in the Big Apple. I know of one case where a real estate broker in a large city quit her job and invested $6,000 in a hot dog pushcart. She now enjoys a greater income than she did in real estate, and doesn't have to worry about the occasional "dry spells" that plague even the best of realtors.

In addition to hot dogs, standard pushcart fare includes pizza, soft drinks, ice cream bars, tamales, soft pretzels, etc. Health permits are required to operate a food pushcart, but that's not an insurmountable obstacle.

Street vending may not be as prestigious as owning a store or other business in a permanent location, but it can be a stepping stone to one. Several successful restaurants and clothing stores in our area can trace their origins back to such humble beginnings.

While my wife and I have never sold on street corners, we aren't totally averse to the idea. In fact, we have a potential location picked out — just in case. We also have the property owner's permission and approval from the local city government ("Go ahead and set up, no license required."). Obtaining both took a grand total of three long-distance telephone calls and a few minutes' time. One might think the location is poor, as it's practically in the middle of nowhere, at the very edge of a small town. There is literally nothing in the area — except entrance and exit ramps for a busy interstate highway, three mini-mart/gas stations, McDonald's, Taco Bell, Dairy Queen, Kentucky Fried Chicken, Burger King, etc. Need I say more?

Arts And Crafts Shows

Recently a customer asked, "Do you work Art In The Park at Grass Valley in July?"

"No way!" I replied. "It's showed-out up there. They must have three shows every weekend, all summer long."

My reply may have been a slight exaggeration, but I doubt it. There are literally thousands of arts and crafts shows throughout the country each year. They may share certain characteristics, but no two are exactly alike.

Some are small, loosely organized (or disorganized) affairs run by local artists. More often than not, these people are just looking for an outlet where they can sell their own arts and crafts. Other shows are large extravaganzas run by highly skilled, professional promoters. They may fill an entire auditorium or convention center, charge a gate fee, and have extensive radio, TV, newspaper and billboard advertising.

The vast majority of shows fall in between these two extremes. Many are sponsored by local art leagues or civic organizations. Some limit exhibitors to fine art only. A few exclude art and permit only handicrafts. Most require the exhibitor to be the original artist, but some permit or even encourage dealers who sell original art or handcrafted items. A few will, quite frankly, accept anyone who fills out an application and pays the entry fee. This doesn't necessarily mean sales will be poor for artists. It can, however, be a bit disconcerting to have the person next to you selling Taiwan toys or eyeglass cleaner!

Generally speaking, arts and crafts sales will be poor when the show is in conjunction with another, *unrelated* event, or when there is a lot of free entertainment. We've worked two such shows and were among the more fortunate exhibitors. We actually grossed enough to recover our show costs. In the first case, most of the people attending came just to drink beer and listen to the rock bands. In the second, they were after the free Cokes and balloons being passed out by various local radio stations. The 70,000 people who attended were totally oblivious to the arts and crafts exhibits. We finally stopped watching for shoplifters shortly before noon. The crowd's attitude seemed to be, "Look, Ma, they're pickin' and grinnin' and givin' away corn dogs down at the KXYZ booth!" Hardly conducive to selling arts and crafts!

Surprisingly, the show that is consistently best for us would seem to be totally unsuited to our merchandise. It's advertised as a combination art show and swap meet and takes place in a small town city park each Labor Day weekend. We tried it several years ago simply because the entry fee was low. The show promoter was one of the most disorganized people I've ever met. Attendance was poor and the vendors offered a real hodge-podge of merchandise. Over two inches of rain on Saturday afternoon didn't help, either. But the bottom line is the few people who attended spent money out of all proportion to their numbers. That has held true every year since. There doesn't seem to be any in-between at this show. Exhibitors either do very well or very poorly. Fortunately, we consistently fall into the former category.

Whenever we tell another exhibitor about a good show, they invariably ask, "Where do you find out about them?" Obviously, word of mouth is the best way, but not the only one. Each state has a tourist bureau which generally has a listing of all major events for the current year. Local Chambers of Commerce are also a good source for information on upcoming shows in a specific area. There are also a number of show guides published throughout the country. Some are too general in their information, while others are very detailed. Many will send a potential subscriber a free sample issue, while others distribute back issues free of charge at larger arts and crafts shows. This enables you to compare several and subscribe to the ones which are best for you. Remember, the more specific the information, the better.

There are undoubtedly some very good guides in other parts of the country, but I'm only familiar with the ones which pertain to California and the Southwest. None of them lists every single show in the area covered. This isn't due to negligence on the editor's part, but rather lack of communication from show promoters. After all, the guides can only list shows they know about. The two we subscribe to are:

Hands On Guide, 255 Cranston Crest, Escondido, California 92025-7037, telephone (619) 747-8206. (Lists a wide variety of show types in Arizona, California, Colorado, Idaho, Nevada, New Mexico, Oregon, Utah, Washington and Wisconsin.)

ShoWhat, 3015 W. Pierce Street, Phoenix, Arizona 85009, telephone (602) 272-8438. (Limited to shows in Arizona, but the editor works a few choice out-of-state shows and gladly shares information on them with subscribers. *ShoWhat* is especially valuable for its no-holds-barred reviews of previous shows.)

As with other publications listed herein, I haven't given subscription rates as they are subject to change due to an increase in postage or printing costs, etc. A telephone call to either publication will get you the current rate.

What do you look for in a show? Obviously, good sales are your first concern. If there isn't a review of a particular show in the guides, talk to artists who have worked it in the past. If you can't find any, try to read between the lines in the show listing. To illustrate how this is done, let's look at some hypothetical listings. My own between-the-lines evaluations appear at the end in parentheses. While they may be overly simplistic, my reviews do give you a rough idea of what to expect.

Strawberry Hill Ladies' Auxiliary Craft Show, July 4-5, Strawberry Hill City Park. Crafts only, no fine art, antiques or swap meet items. $10 donation. Contact Mary at 234-5678 or Phyllis at 345-6789. Preference given to local crafters.

(This show is run by a bunch of little old ladies who don't want any competition for their cutesy-cutesy crafts. They fail to realize their previous poor sales may not be the result of competition. Maybe nobody wants what they have.)

Third Annual Long Valley Arts & Crafts Show, Sept. 3-6, Dwight D. Eisenhower Memorial Park, 5678 Prospect Blvd. Fine art & handicrafts by exhibitor only, no imports or re-sale items. $75 for 15' x 20' space, fee includes city license. Juried by 4 photos, 2 of work, 1 of display, 1 of artist in studio or workshop. Contact Mona Henderson, P.O. Box 567, Long Valley, OR 98765, (123) 765-4321. (Reasonable fee for four-day show, especially if business is good. Space size is generous. Photo requirements reasonable, as some shows have had trouble with exhibitors claiming they made something that was actually imported from Taiwan. A few shows even require artists and craftspersons to demonstrate on site.)

Rembrandt Commemorative Fine Arts Show. Oct. 7-8, Mega-bucks Convention Center, 1234 Financial Plaza Blvd., Newport. Fine arts only. Lots of area advertising. Juried show, send 3 photos. 10' x 10' space, $350. Corner location, $450. *Only* 250 booths available. Contact Seymour Shyster, 5678 Yuppie Blvd., Santa Monica, CA 98765, (714) 123-4567. (Forget it! Only 250 booths at $350 to $450 each? Somebody is going to make a lot of money off this one, but it probably won't be the artists. It may not be Seymour Shyster, either, as he is paying out *big* bucks to rent the convention center.)

As a further example of how to evaluate a show, let's look at hypothetical reviews of the above, along with my own comments in parentheses:

Strawberry Hill Ladies' Auxiliary Craft Show, July 4-5. Only one exhibitor reporting, she was disappointed in sales. Poor attendance, show will probably not be repeated next year. (No kidding on all counts!)

Third Annual Long Valley Arts & Crafts Show, Sept. 3-6. This little show continues to grow, from 25 exhibitors its first year to 40 this year. Of eight reporting, only two disappointed. Others rated show fair to excellent. One says his sales go down each year. (Maybe everyone in the area who wants his art has already bought it.) Three reported sales between one and two grand. Smaller crowd than last year, but more inclined to spend, probably due to improving local economy. Low to medium priced items sold well, higher ticket items soft. Only one of those reporting said he wouldn't return. (This little show is well on its way to being a winner. Pay special attention to the comments on the economy, larger displays and variety. If the economy is better this year, it may improve even more next year. Customers are attracted to large, attractive displays. *Variety creates sales potential for every taste and pocketbook.*)

Rembrandt Commemorative Fine Arts Show. Oct. 7-8. Of 40 artists reporting, only one happy with sales, he did over seven grand. Rest disappointed, felt $5 gate was too much, kept away potential buyers for less expensive works. Poor attendance, whether due to lack of advertising or high gate no one could tell. Promoter conspicuously absent from show floor once it was obvious sales were slow. Seven of those reporting didn't even recoup their show fee. (Quite a difference between Long Valley and this show, which only illustrates that a high show fee is no guarantee of good sales. However, the guy who grossed over $7,000 illustrates one thing: even in the poorest shows, some exhibitors will do very well, while others may do poorly at the best of shows.)

Before going to *any* show, evaluate its potential, and that of your merchandise, realistically. *This evaluation may spell the difference between success and failure BEFORE you pay out show fee.*

If you do crafts, is there really a demand for your particular item? You may love making wooden silhouettes of adorable little duckies with checkered bandannas, but will people in your area buy them? If you live in the Southwest, the answer is no. Make mangy howling coyotes with cowboy bandannas instead. Despite having been around for several years, they still sell extremely well, especially when done in pastel colors. Flop-eared bunnies and Holstein cows are currently popular everywhere, but it's anybody's guess how long the trend will last.

If your fine art has universal appeal, count yourself lucky. Some subjects are mainly regional in appeal. Don't expect to sell a lot of seascapes in Phoenix or Dallas, or cowboy and Indian subjects at a beachside resort. Western art is more popular than ever, but that doesn't necessarily mean it will sell in Philadelphia or Boston. One exception is "End Of The Trail," based on the famous statue of the Indian slumped forward on his tired war pony. After Mt. Rushmore, it's probably the most famous American sculpture of all time. Just about anyone in the United States will recognize it, and many will buy it.

Even considering a new show, we always ask ourselves if we can realistically expect to do 10 times our show fee there. That's a *basic* rule of thumb only, but a good one. Obviously, if you do 10 times a $20 show fee, that's only $200, which isn't enough to make it worthwhile. If the show fee is $500, it's possible to do less than $5,000 and still realize a decent profit. Bear in mind that travel costs and your time have to be considered. If you can gross $1,000 in a show an hour's drive from home, that's better than traveling 1,000 miles each way to gross $3,000.

If a show is brand new, try to evaluate its future potential. Last year, we did a Native American show in the southern part of the state. Our sales *just* made the 10 times guideline. After we paid our travel costs, it wasn't very profitable for us. We plan to return this year, however, as the show has good potential. Our sales would undoubtedly have been much better if the wind hadn't blown at 45-50 mph all day Sunday. Of the seven or eight other vendors who signed up for this first-time event, every one of them stayed set up, despite the heavy winds. That spoke well for the caliber of vendors the show attracted. They were all *pros*. Most plan to return this year, as they believe it could eventually develop into a highly profitable show.

The sponsors (as opposed to professional promoters) had never done a show before and were obviously inexperienced. They weren't lacking in enthusiasm, however, and went out of their way to accommodate the vendors. When one early arrival pointed out a potential problem with canopies blowing over in the wind, they immediately shifted the show from blacktop to dirt so the vendors could stake down. It required rearranging the entire show layout, but it was accomplished within a matter of minutes. When attendance was poor on Saturday, the sponsors stayed up half the night painting more signboards to direct traffic to the show site on Sunday. Their efforts would undoubtedly have paid off if the weather had cooperated. In my opinion, these people deserve another chance, and yet another if that's what it takes to give this show a chance to realize its full potential.

If you want to sell your arts and crafts, but traveling to and from shows and risking bad weather doesn't appeal to you, there is still a viable alternative. In recent years, arts and crafts outlets in storefronts have increased greatly in popularity. In fact, there are actually too many of them in certain areas, but sales can be surprisingly good in some of them.

The concept of these arts and crafts markets is so simple that it's a wonder someone didn't think of it years ago. Basically, an entrepreneur leases a storefront, then subleases space to individual artists and craftspeople for a monthly fee. These spaces may be what is called a gallery wall, which is strictly wall space, or a certain square footage of floor space for free-standing displays. The market's owner and his staff handle all sales, collect the sales tax, and take care of all the normal details of running a business. The individual artist only has to keep his or her display stocked, pay their rent and donate a certain amount of work time each month. This will vary from four hours to a full day each month. The market owner keeps track of all sales and sends his tenants a check every two weeks.

While most of these outlets have a large proportion of crafts, I know of at least one in Scottsdale, Arizona which features mostly fine art and expensive decorator items. The concept is obviously a successful one as they have *very* little turnover in tenants, which is unusual. The owner is a rare combination. He's a professional artist who also has a good head for business. He has an effective advertising campaign and his annual anniversary party consistently attracts a large crowd of Scottsdale's moneyed population. We have a booth in this market and have found it to be profitable. Several of the other tenants actually make a living just off their sales in this one market.

The biggest advantage of any of those arts and crafts markets is that they are open seven days a week, except on holidays. They give you the opportunity to sell your arts and crafts almost every day of the year, rain or shine.

Fairs And Carnivals

Some shadow merchants do extremely well just working fairs and carnivals. If you doubt this, just take a look at the size of some of the motor homes in the exhibitors' overnight parking areas!

Certain items are perpetual moneymakers at these events, no matter what part of the country. Unfortunately, these are generally limited to food items, $2 geegaws and rides.

When fairgoers have a reasonable amount of money to spend, more expensive "pitch" items often sell well. These are items which can be easily demonstrated by anyone who is a smooth talker. Typical pitch items to be found at larger fairs include massaging lounge chairs, eyeglass cleaner, home water softeners and potato peelers that supposedly do everything but shine your shoes, take out the garbage and feed the cat (that model will be out next year). In fact, just about any gimmick that is reasonably to moderately priced can be a successful pitch item at the right fair.

Several vendors at our winter swap meet location work fairs, carnivals and special events in the Midwest during the summer. I can always tell a pitch vendor without even looking at their merchandise. Typically, their booth will be colorful and attractive. They will be wearing a throat mike and will have a line of patter that would do justice to a used car salesman and a politician rolled into one. In other words, you want to believe what you hear, even though you know better.

Many larger fairs have commercial buildings. These are usually the best locations for more expensive items, although some inexpensive souvenir-type items do equally well.

A jury-rigged display that is acceptable for swap meets will definitely *not* work here. All electrical connections, table covers, etc., must be able to pass stringent fire codes. Don't try to cheat on them. The fire marshal *will* be around to check them.

At some smaller fairs, the best commercial spaces will automatically be assigned to local merchants. This may seem unfair, but it's understandable. After all, Henry's Feed & Farm Supply contributes to the local economy all year long, not just on fair weekends.

A novice might assume the largest state fairs with attendance in the millions would be the most lucrative. This isn't necessarily true. When considering a fair, the *paid* gate and fairground acreage are among the most critical factors. As an example, let's look at a hypothetical fair which would seem to offer outstanding possibilities.

The fairground covers 300 acres. During the fair's 14-day run, an estimated 5,000,000 people will attend. Admission is $7.50 for adults, $4 for children under 12, with $3 for parking. That means a family of four will have to spend $26 just to get in the gate. After that, how much will they have left to spend? Probably not much, if they're a typical young family and the local economy is poor. The kids will want to spend what money they have on rides and games. The parents will probably only patronize the hot dog and beer stands.

Remember, these are people who *paid* to get in the gate. They're the ones who are most likely to spend some money once they get inside. As Jim Goodridge, editor of *Fair Times* once said, "I remain committed to the belief that free gates bring free loaders." A large fair will typically hand out several thousand free passes to government officials, the news media, etc. It may also feature a free Kids' Day, Seniors' Day, Fans of Elvis Day or whatever else the fair promoters can dream up to boost overall attendance on slow days. There will also be a certain number of teenagers who will attend every night just for the rides. After all is said and done, the actual paid gate at our hypothetical fair may only be 4,000,000. This still sounds like a lot of people, but how many of them will walk the entire 300 acres?

If you're stuck in a back corner somewhere, which is likely, you may be lucky to have 10,000 people see you during the entire two weeks. Even though your location is poor, you will probably pay just as much for it as you would for a choice spot in a big traffic area. These spots are usually assigned to vendors who have occupied them for years and who often pay for them a full year in advance.

One fellow I know likes to brag that he takes in $30,000 at such-and-such a state fair each year. That sounds like a lot of money, but remember that's his gross. His space rent is $12,000 for the Fair's two-week run. Assuming he's lucky enough to get a tristone, his merchandise costs $10,000. After deducting fees and inventory cost, he has $8,000 left. Out of that, he has to pay his sales tax, help and travel expenses, none of which are cheap. His final net isn't all that high. For the privilege of earning it, he works 12 to 16 hours a day, two weeks straight through. Under those conditions, he's lucky if he makes a decent hourly wage.

The right items *can* be profitable at a large state fair, but you could easily starve to death while trying to find that combination.

By contrast, there are many small fairs where it's possible to realize a decent profit for your investment of time and money. The fees will be much lower, and you will generally only work three or four days without a break. As mentioned earlier, I know several shadow merchants who do very well working county fairs in the Midwest during the summer months. In some cases, a particular fair may be the only major event in the area all year long. People have nowhere else to spend their money. If the fairgrounds are small, there's a very good chance each booth will receive its share of traffic.

My favorite story about small fairs involves a tiny, isolated community in Alaska. It didn't quite take a dog sled to reach it, but almost.

When one carney who ran a game joint on commission saw this town for the first time, she asked a friend, "Why the *#@#% did I let you talk me into this?" Her friend told her to reserve judgment until the end of the first day. At the end of that day, her *commission* from the game receipts was well over $1,000. She later learned that most of the few people in the area made good money working on the nearby oil pipeline. There was nowhere to spend that money — except at the tiny fair once a year.

Of course, the big moneymakers at fairs and carnivals are the carnivals themselves. At larger fairs, it's not at all unusual for one ride or game joint to gross several thousand dollars in a single day. They *have* to do a large gross to be profitable, as most pay a large percentage to the fair promoters. One state fair charges game joints $145 per front foot, with a minimum of 15 feet. On top of that $2,175 base fee, they also charge 60 percent of the gross. So if one joint grossed $10,000 during the fair's run, its owner would only net out $1,825. Out of that, he would have to pay travel expenses, salaries or commissions and replacement cost for any prizes given away.

Food booths also pay premium prices at the larger fairs. I know of one state fair that charges 42 percent of the gross, in addition to the entry fee, temporary health permits, etc. Is it any wonder the equivalent of a 59 cent McDonald's hamburger costs $2 at some fairs?

In summary, it is possible to make a decent living working the fair circuit, but success isn't automatic. It still requires that magic formula of having the right thing at the right price in the right location at the right time — and hope the weather cooperates.

Most state or local Chamber of Commerce offices will have information on upcoming fairs in a specific area. For nationwide information, subscribe to:

Fair Times, P.O. Box 692, Abington, Pennsylvania 19001, telephone (215) 887-5700, ext. 355.

In addition to covering fairs, *Fair Times* carries listings of numerous upcoming specialty shows which might be profitable for a particular shadow merchant. They also publish a handy

Dealer's Desk Reference which contains over 6,000 listings for fairs, festivals and other specialty events during the current calendar year. It could well answer the oft-asked question, "Business is slow in (month), what are we going to do then?"

Gun Shows

For certain types of merchandise, gun shows can be one of the most lucrative markets for shadow merchants. In fact, some of the most successful ones I know work nothing but gun shows.

A popular misconception about gun shows is that they are like museums. There are a lot of guns in glass cases, pretty to look at but *verboten* to touch. Nothing could be further from the truth!

Gun shows are actually marketplaces where dealers and private individuals alike can get together to buy, sell and trade guns and related items. In many cases, a prospective buyer can view and handle several hundred different types of guns in just a few hours. He probably wouldn't find such a variety even if he visited every gun shop in town. He can also find a wide selection of holsters, gun parts, reloading equipment, after-market accessories and gun books.

As with most specialty types, gun shows range from small, locally-organized events held in the high school gymnasium to extravaganzas organized by professional promoters. The latter often fill an entire convention center. One of the biggest is the Great Western in Pomona, California. It features literally acres of tables under roof. Dealers there sell just about every item that could possibly appeal to gun lovers.

Generally speaking, the larger shows are the most lucrative, but there are exceptions. One tiny show in our area is noted for excellent sales. A potential seller literally has to wait for a regular dealer to get sick or die before he can get a table. In another instance, a part-time dealer contracted for a single table at a medium-sized show, hoping to sell a half dozen or so guns. He sold out by noon Friday, then spent the rest of the weekend buying used guns from other dealers and reselling them — at a profit. The concessionaire *thought* he had brought enough hot dogs, buns and soft drinks. He sold out early, and had to re-stock from the local supermarket. At yet another small show, a friend of mine made a $2,000 profit liquidating part of his collection. Not bad for two days' work!

Whether large or small, most gun shows are organized as follows: A promoter will rent exhibit space, banquet tables and folding chairs, etc., for a certain sum. He will then re-rent the tables to various individuals who wish to sell at the show. Depending on a show's size and reputation, the usual fee is from $25 to $100 per 8 foot table in the center of the room. Wall tables are more expensive, but are worth the extra cost due to the additional display space. The promoter then uses his receipts from table rentals to pay for advertising, which can be extensive and expensive. Since he charges admission to the public, it's to his advantage to blitz the show area with advertising. The larger the attendance, the greater his profit.

Some gun shows are limited to guns and gun-related items only. Others permit, or even encourage, dealers to bring knives, coins, military collectibles, western and wildlife art, Indian artifacts and Western Americana. A few of the smaller shows will, quite frankly, allow just about anything that is legal and which the seller lists as "collectibles." This doesn't mean it's a bad show for gun dealers. Promoters hate to have empty tables, as it leaves a bad impression with the public. They would rather rent a table to a collectibles dealer or even give it away to a regular dealer than have it empty. More than once, we've paid for three tables and wound up trying to fill five or six once we got to the show.

Individual show rules will vary, but some are standard at virtually every show. Only security personnel are allowed to carry loaded weapons on the premises, and they check incoming weapons at the door. Loose ammunition and alcoholic beverages are prohibited. Smoking is permitted at a few of the smaller shows, prohibited at most. Of course, all federal, state and local gun laws must be obeyed. Professional dealers selling guns and ammunition are required to have a Federal Firearms License (referred to simply as FFL in the trade). Usually, an individual disposing of a few of his personal guns once or twice a year doesn't have to worry about a license, but local laws will vary.

At larger shows, be prepared to see a few customers and dealers alike dressed as cowboys, mountain men, Civil War soldiers or Rambo. They will usually be armed accordingly, but are hardly to be considered dangerous. They're merely indulging in harmless flights of fantasy. Their Walter Mitty trip is one way of temporarily escaping the pressures of our modern society. It may or may not be cheaper than visiting a psychiatrist, but it's a lot more fun!

When we first became shadow merchants, I wanted to try gun shows, but my wife didn't. She was probably afraid I would spend all our profits buying guns ("But honey, the guy only wants two grand for the Colt General Custer carried at the Little Big Horn!"). Actually, she had nothing to worry about. Her attitude changed drastically after she talked to a friend at our winter market. "I work a few gun shows in the summer with my Indian jewelry," she said. "Men often bring their entire families, and there's nothing to appeal to the wives and kids." Bingo! My wife suddenly got the brilliant idea of working gun shows. After all, we could easily qualify in the Western Americana category.

Our winter season was rapidly drawing to a close, so we opted to try a gun show the last weekend in April. Plan B would have been to try squeezing one more weekend out of the swap meet. The gun show wasn't especially lucrative for us, but it did give us a chance to get our feet wet in a previously untried marketplace. It also proved to be a wise decision for that particular weekend. While the swap meet vendors sweltered in record heat, we were outselling them in a nice, cool exhibit hall. We also didn't have to spend two hours setting up in the morning and another two hours tearing down at night. At the end of the day on Saturday, we simply threw dust covers over our table and walked out the door. On Sunday morning, it took us about five minutes to remove the covers and be ready for business.

That first show was an education, and gave me an idea whereby my knowledge of leatherwork could be put to good use. A couple of dealers were selling handmade replicas of Old West-style holsters. The quality wasn't bad, but their prices were outrageous. Prior to the next gun show, I made up a couple of dozen holsters for several popular handguns. Since one out of every six Americans is a southpaw, I concentrated on that market. My "Leather for Lefties" display got a lot of attention at the next couple of shows, and I sold several holsters there. I kept my prices somewhat lower than the going rate for good commercial holsters, and considerably lower than the Old West offerings mentioned previously. I'll never be a threat to the major manufacturers, but was able to turn a little spare time and materials into money in my pocket.

Surprisingly, the most lucrative gun show we ever worked was in an out-of-the-way town that is famous for only one thing. It consistently rivals Death Valley for the nation's hot spot in the summer. The promoter spent a great deal of money for a two-hour live remote broadcast on the local country music station. I was one of a half-dozen dealers interviewed. Within an hour, customers were asking for specific items I had mentioned on the radio. At the end of the show, we were able to attribute over $500 in sales directly to the broadcast. If a gun show promoter asks you to participate in a live remote broadcast, don't hesitate — go for it! If you are interested in working gun shows, the local gun shop will probably have information on upcoming shows in your area. For future listings nationwide, I strongly recommend the following publications:

Gun Show Calendar, 700 East State St., Iola, Wisconsin 54990, telephone (715) 445-2214. (Published quarterly, it's virtually the bible of gun show information.)

The Shotgun News, Snell Publishing Co., PO Box 669, Hastings, Nebraska 68902, telephone (402) 463-4589. (Published three times monthly. It contains literally thousands of classified and display ads for virtually every type of product or service associated with guns and shooting.)

One last word on gun shows. The vast majority of promoters and dealers alike are scrupulously honest. However, an occasional nefarious character slips in now and then. If someone *should* offer you the Colt Custer carried at the Little Big Horn, avoid him like the plague! Custer was actually carrying a brace of nickel-plated English revolvers. These guns still exist, but they aren't likely to turn up at a gun show. I know roughly where they are, and will only say they are still considered "spoils of war." However, I must admit I was sorely tempted to reach for my wallet at a gun show last year. Another dealer had a Colt that had belonged to Buffalo Bill Cody. *That* one was accompanied by a letter of authenticity from the Colt factory.

Special Interests = Special Events

Name just about any hobby or sport that appeals to the human race and there is likely a show, convention or rally that appeals to people with that interest. Many of these gatherings offer a golden opportunity for shadow merchants to make money, especially for those who cater to a select clientele. Some travel the rodeo or horse show circuits full-time and do extremely well. Others may only work a handful of smaller events each year. For them, specialized sales is either a way of supporting their hobby or of supplementing the income from a full-time job.

Mention the Black Hills of South Dakota and most people immediately think of Mt. Rushmore or Deadwood, the former boom town where Wild Bill Hickok and Calamity Jane are buried. But to any biker worth his Harley T-shirt, mention of the Black Hills automatically means Sturgis. During the first week of August each year, the surrounding hills reverberate with the roaring engines of Harleys, Gold Wings, Kawasakis and Triumphs as thousands of bikers descend on the small community of Sturgis. The number will vary from year to year, but there are usually between 100,000 and 500,000 bikers in attendance. While a few are pure scum looking for trouble, the vast majority just want a chance to relax and do their own thing. Many have good jobs and spend their money freely. I know several shadow merchants who wouldn't think of working anywhere but Sturgis in August. They obviously gear their merchandise toward bikers, with items such as T-shirts/leather jackets and certain types of jewelry selling well. Needless to say, the emerald bracelet that would sell in Beverly Hills isn't what you take to Sturgis. Slave bracelets, pendants and rings featuring eagles, cobras and skulls are more appropriate for a biker crowd, although some bikers appreciate good Indian pawn jewelry and will pay the price for it.

What Sturgis is to bikers, Oshkosh, Wisconsin is to aviation enthusiasts. Each year, the annual Experimental Aircraft Association fly-in at Oshkosh draws a crowd of several hundred thousand. Virtually every type of aircraft imaginable can be seen there, with warbirds of World War Two vintage always attracting a crowd. Harley T-shirts and belt buckles might not sell at Oshkosh, but those depicting pre-war Stinsons and Beeches or World War Two fighters certainly should.

I once met a fellow who claimed he did extremely well just selling antique license plates and glass-domed gas pumps. He said it didn't matter whether he worked an antique auto auction or a hot rod show, those items sold well. Remember, the more unique your merchandise, the better your chances of making money, so long as it's appropriate to a particular crowd. Cookbooks would obviously be a lost cause at a car show, but decoupage plaques of pre-1970s car ads from now-defunct magazines such as *Collier's* might be a hot item.

For a *really* unusual event, consider working Oklahoma's annual rattlesnake roundup, which is exactly what the name implies. A cookbook featuring various ways of preparing rattlesnake meat just might be the ticket, provided you can stomach the research (pun intended). *Don't* expect to make a killing with rattlesnake belt buckles, wallets, cigarette cases or hatbands. They will probably be in abundance everywhere.

If you are an avid sports fan, consider working sports memorabilia shows. Don't just order a bunch of baseball cards or team-licensed caps and jackets from a wholesaler. There will already be a number of dealers selling them because they are easy to obtain. Do consider a used paperback setup specializing in books by or about famous athletes. There should be a demand for them. The main problem will be getting and maintaining a decent inventory.

Indian powwows generally limit their vendors to Native Americans with an official Bureau of Indian Affairs tribal registration number, but not always. My wife and I recently worked a couple of non-exclusive powwows with our Indian art. While sales weren't great at either one, they were still worthwhile.

Occasionally, a seemingly unrelated item *will* sell well at a specialized event. Last summer, we took our Indian art to a four-day archery shoot. It turned out to be the most lucrative event we worked the entire summer. A friend did equally well with wildlife T-shirts and her daughter sold out her entire inventory of toys the first day. The event's promoters were obviously correct in their assumption that a new dealer selling non-archery items would do well. Needless to say, we plan to make the archery shoot an annual event in our summer schedule.

The list of specialized shows and events is virtually endless. There are antique and glassware shows, teddy bear doll shows, model railroad meets, gem and mineral shows, hot air balloon races, science fiction and comic book conventions, mountain man rendezvous and many, many more. Many smaller communities have annual events such as duck races, jumping frog contests, pumpkin or strawberry festivals and the like. Some of these can be very lucrative while others are relatively poor for sales. Yet each affords an enterprising shadow merchant the opportunity to expand his or her selling horizons.

When choosing a specialized field in which to sell, try to keep potential customers' budgets in mind. Antique car auctions, horse shows and lodge conventions will generally attract a more affluent crowd who will buy high-ticket items. Many of the people attending science fiction or comic book conventions will be teenagers with a limited amount of money to spend. In such cases, lower-priced items usually sell best. Remember what I said in the chapter entitled "When to Diversify" concerning items priced under $10 or over $40!

Last but not least, when working special interest shows, learn as much about that interest as you possibly can. *This is especially imperative — you gear your merchandise to that particular crowd.* If selling older, truly collectible baseball cards, it would behoove you to know that Joe wasn't the only DiMaggio to grace the diamond. Brothers Dominic and Vince contributed their share to the game's lore. If you sell model railroad cars, be prepared to offer to change Kaydee to Rapido couplers, and vice versa. Also know the differences between O, S, HO, and Z scales. In short, do your homework! It will pay off in the long run.

A Storefront Without
A Storefront

In the preceding chapters, my emphasis was on retailing without a storefront, generally outdoors. It still is. However, it's time to look at storefronts that aren't really storefronts, yet offer certain advantages common to them.

Sometimes described as pushcarts without wheels or glorified newsstands, kiosks have enjoyed increasing popularity among small retailers in recent years. For those unfamiliar with the term, the above descriptions aren't entirely accurate or complimentary. Kiosks are actually small, free-standing stands or display areas which can be closed up at the end of the selling day. Many are quite attractive. They are basically temporary sales outlets, although many are set up in permanent or semi-permanent locations, principally inside shopping malls.

Operating a kiosk in a mall has several advantages. First, with the national average for vacancies presently running about 10 percent, many mall owners are willing to negotiate attractive, short-term leases for kiosks. This allows a budding entrepreneur to lease space in an area he might not otherwise be able to afford. It also gives mall owners a chance to increase their income. Additionally, they know a kiosk owner who is successful may eventually decide to lease a storefront on a long-term basis. While kiosk leases generally run for six months to a year, a storefront lease is for five to ten years.

Second, a kiosk owner doesn't have to invest a fortune in store fixtures. A very attractive kiosk can be built for anywhere from a couple of hundred to several thousand dollars. The actual cost is determined by how elaborate it is and how much of the work the owner can do himself.

Third, it costs far less to stock a kiosk than it does a storefront. The average kiosk is 100 square feet or less, yet offers adequate display for small items when properly designed. An inventory that will completely fill the average kiosk would be lost in a storefront.

Fourth, a vacant storefront which might be available in a busy mall may be located far from the heaviest foot traffic. A kiosk, on the other hand, is usually placed in an open area where a large number of people are bound to see it. In some of the larger malls, one owner may operate two or three kiosks in separate areas, with each selling different merchandise.

Fifth, a kiosk offers more prestige than a swap meet or street corner location. It sounds better to say you sell at Pine Bluff mall rather than at Big John's Swap Meet or the corner of Fifth and Grand, even if it may not actually be more profitable.

Sixth, an indoor kiosk can remain open even during inclement weather, just like a regular storefront. That can be an important factor *anywhere* in the country, no matter what the Chamber of Commerce claims about the local weather.

In addition to malls, kiosks may be located in the lobbies of motels or resort hotels or gambling casinos. Either location offers good foot traffic, with the patrons generally being more affluent than those found in malls.

There are, of course, some disadvantages to kiosks. Chief among these is their size. The choice of merchandise is limited to smaller items unless you want to limit your display to a few large items. Remember, that also limits your sales potential. Some customers may shy away from buying more expensive merchandise at kiosks due to their temporary appearance. They may feel they will have no recourse if the merchandise is defective and the kiosk and its owner suddenly vanish. Space rent for a kiosk can be high as compared to outdoor locations, but it may be worth it in the long run. In a couple of cases, I talked to kiosk owners who pay no base rent, but pay the landlord a percentage of their gross sales each week. This arrangement seemed to satisfy both parties.

Small items which can be sold in a kiosk are limited only by the owner's imagination. These might include family coat of arms, gift baskets, regional souvenirs, dried flower arrangements, music boxes, belts and buckles, incense and potpourri, team-licensed sports products and a myriad of other things. One fellow I used to know made custom redwood signs while the customer waited at his outdoor kiosk. He operated in the same summer resort location for 19 years and was able to make a living for the entire year in just a few months' time.

As with any other sales location for shadow merchants, a kiosk can be an end in itself or it can be a stepping stone to other things. More than one kiosk owner has gone on to open a store or even a chain of stores which was successful. Remember, whatever your present situation, your future is limited only by the scope of your imagination and your willingness to work in order to make that dream come true.

Off-Season Markets

Some shadow merchants are fortunate enough to do well, or at least make a living, in one outdoor location throughout the year. The vast majority, however, are forced to change locations with the seasons. After all, who would want to shop outdoors in Michigan in December, or under the blistering Arizona sun in July?

As mentioned previously, many vendors at our winter location are from the Midwest. They work fairs and special events during the summer, then head for the Sun Belt as winter approaches. For them, winter is the "off" season. For us, the exact opposite applies. During our first three years in business, it wasn't unusual for one month's sales in February or March to exceed our total gross for May through September. By the very nature of our business, we're limited to working close to home and our sources of supply. We simply aren't able to travel to the more lucrative Eastern summer markets. It's taken several years to work out a schedule where we at least have a chance of making an adequate living in the summer months, but it's finally an accomplished fact. We still have some very slow summer weekends, but fortunately they are outnumbered by others that range from adequate to downright good, even by winter standards.

Looking back on our first winter season, I still marvel at how good our sales were. A combination of beginner's luck, hard work and a sound economy were definitely in our favor. Despite our success, we were well aware the season wouldn't last forever. By early March, we were asking seasoned veterans where they worked in the summer. Most went to the Midwest, but two or three recommended we try a certain swap meet in a neighboring state. "If you think you did well here, wait until you get to Bluff City," one said.

Our friends meant well, but neglected to tell us that Bluff City (not its real name) was only good from the middle of July until Labor Day weekend. We drastically expanded our inventory and headed for Bluff City early in May. Sales were poor the first weekend, but we blamed it on the bad weather. "People have had a chance to see us, so sales should be better next week," we told ourselves. The bubble soon burst, as our gross went down the following weekend, and again the week after. We finally saw the light when I totaled up our sales for the month. In five weekends, we had grossed only a few dollars more than on the final Sunday of the winter season! Our best weekend in Bluff City brought in just enough money to pay travel expenses, with nothing left over for restocking or our living expenses.

With starvation just around the corner, it was obvious a plan would have to be devised *immediately!* Having a Plan C worked out wouldn't hurt, either.

Fortunately, we remembered that a winter neighbor worked a small swap meet in the summer which was only a couple of hours' drive from our home. We had his telephone number, so we called to see how he was doing. "It's still slow," he said, "but there's never much business in Pinedale until June. You should at least make grocery and rent money there. You might even do well, as there's nobody there with your type of merchandise."

Since the following weekend fell at the first of June, we decided to try Pinedale. We reserved a room at the motel our friend recommended, loaded the truck with merchandise, and drove up on Friday afternoon. We knew the swap meet was on dirt, in the parking area of a small drive-in theater, but who cared as long as business was good?

Unfortunately, sales were poor that first weekend. On Saturday, we only sold enough to pay our space rent. Sunday was better, but still somewhat less than mediocre. Having been burned badly at Bluff City, it would have been easy to give up after that first weekend. Two factors, however, convinced us to try Pinedale at least once more. First, I recognized several vendors from our winter market. A couple of them told me they worked Pinedale every summer. Second, the people walking through the swap meet appeared, in general, to be more prosperous than those in Bluff City. Surely they would have more disposable income to spend on Indian art.

Although sales weren't spectacular our second weekend, they were far better than the first. We wound up returning to

Pinedale every weekend through September, with just a couple of exceptions. We tried Bluff City once again in July, only to repeat our previous disappointing sales. A couple of weeks later, we went to the West Coast for one weekend. People at the large swap meet we tried liked our merchandise, but they didn't buy. When we considered the difference in travel expenses, Pinedale began to look especially good to us. We were at least selling enough there to buy groceries, pay the rent, and partially restock our inventory.

Fortunately, the Terrific Twins were operating a second unit for us in Wisconsin that summer. Their sales varied greatly from week to week, but we did make a small profit on their unit which helped pay the bills. We still had a decent inventory as we approached our second winter, and had only accumulated a light debt load during the summer.

As our second summer season approached, we were still naive enough to believe we could make money from other units. The details of that fiasco were covered in "Other People, Other Units." We had stripped our own inventory drastically and had also gone heavily into debt to supply those units. Needless to say, our own sales in Pinedale were mediocre at best until we began pulling merchandise from the other units. Invariably, our sales increased dramatically the weekend after we stripped one of them. We also increased our sales by adding in the nickel and dime section described in "When To Diversify." Despite posting a 10 percent gain over the preceding summer, we entered fall on the verge of bankruptcy. The increase in sales just hadn't been enough to pay off creditors from the previous spring.

Fortunately, our fall sales picked up much sooner than anticipated. For a couple of years, we had been hearing about a large swap meet at Arroyo Verde, in another part of the state. Near the end of that second summer in Pinedale, I learned that a neighboring vendor had occasionally worked Arroyo Verde, so

I pressed him for details. "It's hot, dusty and the hours are long, but you should make money there," he said. We decided to try it the first weekend of October. It *was* hot and dusty, and the hours *were* long, but business was very good for that time of year. On Saturday, we literally made our last sale of the day at 11:15 that night! We stayed at Arroyo Verde through the second weekend of November. We undoubtedly would have done very well later than that, but it was time to return to our regular winter location.

Thanks to our good sales at Arroyo Verde, plus a large Christmas order from France, we were finally able to see a little light at the end of the financial tunnel. We no longer discussed bankruptcy, even in theoretical terms, but began working even harder to get creditors paid off that winter. We didn't quite erase our debt load, but did reduce it enough so creditors could tell we were making a sincere effort to get them paid in full. Their attitudes toward us changed, as they knew what a severe financial beating we took the previous summer.

At the start of our third summer, we decided to try our winter market's sister swap meet in a nearby city. It was much larger, and supposedly business was reasonably good even in the summer. It would be a lot hotter than Pinedale, but would be close enough to home so we could commute each day. The first two weekends, sales were encouraging if not spectacular. The third weekend was excellent. When the full force of the summer heat arrived on the fourth weekend, sales nosedived right into the ground. "If we're going to starve, let's do it in Pinedale where it's cool," we said. We spent the rest of the summer there, with two weekends out to work gun shows closer to home.

By the end of September, we had posted a 13 percent increase over the previous summer. Although money was tight, we were at least eating three meals a day.

Toward the end of the fourth winter season, another vendor began bragging about how well he did in California art shows during the summer. We agreed to meet him at one show on the coast for Memorial Day weekend, working Arroyo Verde the first three weekends in May. We hadn't heard from our friend in California, but assumed he was doing well. It was a distinct shock when we finally saw him Memorial Day. "Go back home and stay there," he said. "It's dead here." Other people at the show repeated his tale of woe. The main topics of conversation were the severe drought and the additional 600,000 people who would be out of work by the end of the year. When we had no trouble finding a parking place for our big Supercab right on the harbor, we *knew* the economy was bad. Normally, the area would have been packed with tourists over Memorial Day.

We returned to Arroyo Verde the following weekend. Despite the heat, sales were good enough that we stayed for all of June. We finally left when the summer monsoons came to the desert. It proved to be a wise move that particular summer. We weren't rained out even once in Pinedale, but Arroyo Verde was soaked almost every weekend from the middle of July until after Labor Day.

We also tried several art shows that summer. They were unknown factors, as we had yet to discover the show guides recommended in the chapter on arts and crafts shows. Two of the shows were disasters, but we did very well at three others. All in all, we posted a 56 percent increase over the previous summer, almost doubling our sales from our first summer. During that fourth year in business, six of the twelve months were our best ever for that particular month. Of those, five were posted during the slow summer season. Obviously, we had finally discovered a combination of swap meets and shows that would produce acceptable summer sales.

Our sales continued to increase every summer until last year, when they dropped 14 percent. It would be easy to blame the especially wet monsoon season, or the fact we decided not to work four different weekends in August and September. On closer examination, however, our records show the largest downturn for a single month was in June, *before* the monsoons arrived. We also had a valid reason for not working the four weekends we chose. Experience clearly demonstrated those particular weekends were consistently slow, no matter where we had worked in previous years. It simply didn't make any sense to work all weekend, liquidating merchandise just to pay travel expenses. It's one thing to take a chance on an unknown factor that might prove profitable, but quite another to waste your time, energy and money fighting against losing odds.

The real surprise concerning our summer sales decline is reflected in our records for the calendar year. Despite several record-setting months, our sales for the entire year were down 14 percent, the same figure as for the summer months. This suggests the sluggish national economy, especially for a Presidential election year, might have been the real culprit.

While our off-season sales are still much lower than in the winter, they have finally evened out enough so we can survive the lean summer months. Despite last year's decline, we anticipate an increase this coming summer. Just how much of an increase we see will depend on the three key factors that *always* influence sales. These are the state of the national and local economies, the weather, and our own determination to make it happen.

One Final Note Of Caution: Remember, what sells well at one location may sell poorly at another, and vice versa. It may be necessary to make some changes in your inventory when going from Market A to Market B. This is true regardless of the distance between them. Remain as flexible as possible in both choice of merchandise and choice of location. There is a lot of truth to the old proverb that the tree which survives the storm is the one that can bend with the wind.

Beware The High Rent District

Usually, junk mail is nothing but a nuisance, destined for a quick trip to the round file. Occasionally, however, it contains a few laughs.

In early October of last year, we received a flier promoting a so-called retail sales extravaganza scheduled for the upcoming Thanksgiving weekend. As I read through it, I realized the *minimum* space into which we could fit an effective display would *only* cost us $1,800! When a representative of the show called a few days later, the conversation went something like this:

"Hello, this is Mark Smoothie of Megabucks Extravaganzas, Inc. Did you receive our flier for the Thanksgiving show at the Midas Convention Center?"

"We sure did," I replied, "and I wouldn't touch it with a ten-foot pole."

After a few seconds of dead silence, good ol' Mark recovered his composure sufficiently to inquire, rather incredulously, exactly why I didn't think he was offering me the opportunity of a lifetime. After all, the Friday after Thanksgiving was only the biggest shopping day of the year.

"First of all, your rent's outrageous," I informed him. "The barest minimum space we would need would cost us nearly two grand. Even then, we couldn't put a large enough display to ensure really good sales. Frankly, I think we'd be lucky to make our show fee back. Second, the trend in Christmas shopping has shifted dramatically in the last few years. People now tend to do their Christmas shopping later and later, and spend more money for a last-minute gift than they would have just a few weeks earlier. Frankly, we'll probably sell just as much at the swap meet we normally work, and with a lot less overhead."

Mark could see he wasn't going to get anywhere with me, so he quickly hung up and called his next prospect. As luck would have it, the weather was miserable Thanksgiving weekend, so sales were poor at the swap meet. We did, however, realize a small profit. When we finally began receiving reports on the Megabucks show, however, we knew we had made the right decision. Over the next several months, we talked to at least a half dozen people who had worked the show. One said he had done well, and knew of another who was happy with his sales. The remainder, however, had been ready to lynch the promoter.

His promised advertising blitz never materialized. As a result, attendance was poor and sales were even worse. More than one show participant said he or she wasn't even able to recoup the show fee. One of the primary laws of shadow merchandising was again proven true: A *high space rent or show fee is no assurance of proportionately high sales.* In fact, sales might actually be quite poor by *any* standards.

Unfortunately, many shadow merchants tend to ignore this basic fact. Novices are the worst victims of a glib sales pitch, but seasoned pros are also vulnerable. Remember, any deal that seems too good to be true is usually just that. If it was truly as good as it sounds, the largest, most successful shadow merchants would have it locked up and deposited in Fort Knox within hours after they learned of its existence.

Aside from the large, one-time or annual extravaganzas, the worst offenders at charging too much are probably indoor swap meets in the Southwest. While these markets have been common in Eastern states for years, mainly due to inclement weather, they have only recently begun to appear in significant numbers in sunnier climes. Very few survive more than a year or two.

Several years ago, my wife and I learned that an indoor swap meet was slated to open in a large city near our hometown. Its grand opening was scheduled for the first weekend of October. I knew from experience that business outdoors would be slow then due to lingering summer heat, so we decided to at least investigate the indoor location. Quite frankly, I don't remember exactly how much the space rent was, but it was expensive. When I commented on this, the leasing agent replied, "We have no trouble getting it in New Jersey." I cautioned him that our area wasn't New Jersey, but I don't think he got the message.

To make a long story short, we declined a lease with him and took our chances outdoors. However, we always wondered how the vendors were doing there. We finally got a chance to visit the location the following spring. As it was the very end of the winter season, our business had fallen off drastically. Since sales were quite poor on Friday and Saturday, we decided to take Sunday off and observe the indoor swap meet in operation.

Although we arrived fairly late on Sunday morning, there was a significant lack of foot traffic. That wouldn't have surprised us outdoors, as the weather was blistering hot, but why weren't people shopping in cool, air-conditioned comfort? It certainly wasn't due to lack of advertising. The owners were currently running an extensive TV and newspaper ad campaign. Could it be people in our area just weren't used to indoor swap meets? Was it located too close to the largest shopping mall in the state, which was only a few blocks away? Were the middle-class residents of the area the type who normally disdained swap meets in the first place? Was there a noticeable lack of appealing merchandise to inspire shoppers to return again and again? As it usually takes more than a single factor to make or break a business, a qualified "yes" would probably answer any of the above questions.

We soon located a booth which sold merchandise similar to ours, so we began questioning the proprietress regarding winter sales. She told us business had been pretty good during the winter months, but she was a "little" disappointed in April. To date, her gross receipts were only twice the cost of her space rent. She was flabbergasted when we informed her we were leaving our winter market that weekend because our sales had dropped to four times our space rent. To her "That's bad?" we replied, "My dear, at the height of the season the better vendors complain if they only do *ten* times their space rent." The poor lady was still trying to scrape her jaw off the floor as we walked away.

At this point, I must confess that even old hands like the Coopers can occasionally be lured into a deal that looks promising, but which is doomed to failure from the start.

Just a few weeks before visiting the indoor swap meet chronicled above, we investigated a new outdoor marketplace which would be opening the following winter. On the surface, it had distinct possibilities. There was nowhere to shop within 10 or 12 miles, unless you counted the Mercedes dealership just down the road. There was nothing for people in the area to do, except visit the nearby tennis ranch or attend any one of numerous horse shows. There weren't too many houses nearby, but their prices started at $200,000 and went as high as $1.5 million. In other words, the market's owners weren't exactly trying to attract their clientele from the ghetto!

The facility itself was outstanding, with the owners furnishing very heavy duty canopies for the vendors. Back booths even had a ceiling fan for air circulation during hot weather. Forget the idea of a beer stand offering only one or two brands, customers could actually relax in a quiet lounge area and order mixed drinks from a full-service bar. If a potential tenant was worried about competition, he or she was assured there were limits on just how many could sell the same type of merchandise. The owners also strongly discouraged the use of phony come-ons such as "50% Off" or "Wholesale To The Public" signs.

Of course, there was a price to pay for all these luxuries, and it added up to $75 per day for a 20 x 20 foot space. There was no such thing as trying it for one day or a single weekend; vendors (who were dubbed "shopkeepers") were obligated to sign a month-to-month lease. We initially rejected the idea of leasing there due to the high cost. But as the months rolled by, we kept remembering what a friend had told us about a swap meet he used to work. It, too, had been located in an exclusive area near high-priced homes. According to our friend, it wasn't unusual for some of the better vendors to gross $12,000 in a single good weekend!

We finally decided the new facility had the potential to be almost as good, so we went ahead and signed on the dotted line. The grand opening, with all its attendant hoopla, attracted a large crowd for the time of year. Considering it was the first weekend in October, sales were pretty good, but not good enough to warrant the high space rent. As the weeks rolled by, sales for most vendors steadily declined. A few did extremely well, but the majority were constantly operating at a loss. We left after the first month, and were soon followed by several others. A few eternal optimists with outside income stayed until the bitter end, which came the following March.

I could offer any number of reasons, all valid, why this facility failed, but basically I think the concept was just ahead of its time. If it had opened five years later with lower space rent, it might have been the forerunner of a nationwide trend.

To date, no one has tried to repeat the ambitious concept described above. There are, however, at least two or three new indoor swap meets opening in the nearby metropolitan area each year. No matter what their location or marketing strategy, they all have two problems in common: the space rent is too high and there is a noticeable lack of foot traffic, at least in comparison to outdoor swap meets.

Last summer, a friend of ours leased space in an indoor show which had been in operation for over a year. He did reasonably well for the first few weekends, then his sales dropped drastically. In desperation, he emptied his warehouse and ran a giant clearance sale. He reduced his already low selling prices by 50 percent or more. His gross sales were fantastic the next weekend, but his profit margin was borderline at best. Since he was on a short-time lease, he was able to pull out shortly thereafter.

A few weeks later, he decided to reexamine the market as a potential fall location. He asked us to join him there, as he wisely wanted a second opinion. We walked through and examined each booth with a critical eye. "There are about two or three real pros in the whole place," we told him. "We saw a handful of young people who are obviously trying their first business venture. Quite likely, either the husband or wife works at a regular job while the other is trying to get a business started. The rest of the tenants are obviously retirees with outside income. There's simply no way you could make a full-time living here."

Several months later, we learned many of the tenants we had seen were not renewing their leases. As one pulled out, a new one would move into their booth. The market's leasing agents were obviously signing them up without regard to their potential for becoming long-term tenants. After all, their commissions were based on how many new tenants they signed up, not renewals. The percentage of turnovers was obviously quite high.

By contrast, there is actually very little turnover of vendors at our winter location. I would say the figure is probably less than 10 percent annually. While some whose sales are marginal simply close up shop and fade into the sunset, the two greatest causes of vendor turnover appear to be death and serious illness. This isn't too surprising when one considers that a few are octogenarians!

Actually, it's fairly easy to tell when an indoor swap meet is in trouble. If the leasing agent calls a few months after your initial contact and offers you a reduced rate, look out. It happened to a friend of ours, and he could hardly wait to share a good laugh with us.

We had visited the facility which offered him a discount several months previously, more out of curiosity than for any other reason. We did, however, walk through the door with open minds regarding its potential. Another friend had told us of one vendor who was doing quite well there, citing actual sales figures to prove his point, so we decided to at least look at the place.

As luck would have it, three other shadow merchants from our winter location arrived just a few minutes after us. The leasing agent was therefore able to make his presentation to five potential tenants, representing our distinctly different businesses, at the same time. It was glossy, to say the least. After consulting with the lady at the turnstile, he was able to tell us exactly how many people had come through the door the preceding weekend. The figure would have been unimpressive in the winter, but was perfectly acceptable for the hot summer. Out of that number, he explained, a certain percentage would actually have money in their pockets for serious shopping. Of these, yet another small percentage might be interested in any given type of merchandise. Both figures were perfectly believable. In short, the guy had done his homework.

After explaining the leasing requirements, he invited us to view videotapes of the TV commercials the facility was currently running on three local channels. I've had my share of experience writing, producing and directing TV spots, so was able to judge them from a professional point of view. Although obviously produced on a low budget, they were first-rate. They would definitely attract the viewer's attention without insulting his or her intelligence.

The presentation proceeded amicably enough until we all began to question if it was possible to gross ten times the space rent there ($4 per square foot per month, versus the 50¢ per square foot we pay at our outdoor location). Where did we get *that* figure, the leasing agent must have wondered. He remained civil enough, but was now obviously viewing us as a bunch of amateurs whose expectations were too high. Actually, we were all experienced pros who were only being realistic. After all, what's the point of leasing space in any given location, no matter how impressive, if you can't make a decent profit? He should have realized just how professional we were when my wife asked if he was set up to process credit card sales electronically. "Doesn't anyone here take MasterCard, VISA, American Express or Discover?" she asked. "We do." Even dropping that hot potato into his lap didn't alter his low opinion of us.

As we drove home, my wife and I chuckled at just how low that opinion was, when compared to reality. As mentioned previously, we live in what could be described as the country club district of our area. At a wholesale gift show only a couple of weeks earlier, one of the other vendors had proceeded to literally buy out two entire booths — for cash on the barrelhead. We know, because we were there. And if Mr. Snooty had bothered to look out his office window, he would have seen the remaining two vendors driving off in a Cadillac limousine!

In some sections of the country, indoor swap meets may be a viable proposition for novice and veteran shadow merchants alike. In the Southwest, however, they just don't offer the sales potential to justify the high space rent. Remember the general rule of thumb: *Gross sales must be at least ten times the space rent.*

To reiterate the immortal words of Wallace as spoken in "Sell What You Like:" "Never mind what your gross is, what's your net? N-E-T, net." Don't just remember those words, chisel them on stone in your mind. If the net profit isn't there, the business won't be there for long.

Murphy Works Overtime

Being Irish, Murphy is a real fun guy. He is also world famous, being to everyday life what Newton was to physics or Einstein to relativity. For the one or two people who are unfamiliar with it, Murphy's Law simply states, "What can go wrong, will." There are infinite variations, many applying to specific professions or activities. Some of the following examples may seem far-fetched, but virtually every shadow merchant I know will swear each is true.

It never rains on Tuesday, only on Friday, Saturday and Sunday. Of course, if your busiest selling day is normally Tuesday, it *only* rains on Tuesday.

You decide to try a new item which may or may not sell well. The first weekend, you have 5 and sell 3 of them. The next weekend, you have 3 dozen, but don't sell any because you don't have a decent selection.

Your helper is always late for work, except that day when you're late. Then he shows up a half hour early.

You never have to leave your setup to go to the bank, Post Office or supermarket — until the day you hire a totally inexperienced helper.

Never get into the express lane at the bank, Post Office or supermarket. That's where *they* put *their* trainees.

A customer's check never bounces, except when you count on it to make a late payment to the IRS.

Always take an umbrella, raincoat and galoshes to work on a sunny day. It never rains on days that start out overcast.

Always listen to the weatherman — and prepare for the opposite type of weather.

On the slowest selling days, customers only come when you are trying to eat lunch or desperately need to go to the restroom.

None of your competitors carries an item you just *know* will be a runaway bestseller. The day you add it to your inventory, they all have it at a lower price.

You mail checks to two different suppliers. The little bitty one you mail across town won't come back to your bank for at least a month. The great big one, which is mailed across the country and you can't cover until next week, will hit your account within 48 hours.

Always take a good book to work. You will only forget it on a slow day when there are no customers.

You need to hire, sight unseen, an assistant to help you sell biker clothing and accessories. You know nothing about them except their names. Rocky Macho turns out to be a former hairdresser who loves ballet. Percy Pipsqueak is an ex-Marine unarmed combat instructor who looks like Rambo's big brother. Not necessarily his older brother, but his B-I-G brother.

No matter how large it is, your new pickup, cargo van or merchandise trailer is an inch too short and too narrow for your actual needs.

Sales are poor at any given time in direct proportion to how desperately you need the money.

Last, but certainly not least, is the most important law of all: *Murphy was an optimist.*

YOU WILL ALSO WANT TO READ: